IDLE RICH
in Spain

A Serial Underachiever's Fresh Start in Andalucía

RICHIE BANNISTER

Text copyright ©2024 Richie Bannister

The author has asserted his moral right under the Copyright, Designs and Patents Act, 1988, to be identified as the author of this work.

All rights reserved. No part of this publication may be reproduced, stored in a retrieval system, or transmitted, in any form or by any means, without the prior permission in writing of the publisher.

1 – Life Before Spain

For a long time I, Richie Bannister, considered myself to be a thoroughly idle man, so when my sister flippantly christened me Idle Rich at the age of forty-six I didn't take offence. After underachieving at school I'd proceeded to drift from job to job, always searching for a congenial occupation which wouldn't overly strain my body or mind. Finally, at the age of thirty-nine – just after my relationship with an attractive and solvent young teacher had petered out, due, she said, to my astounding lack of commitment – I finally stumbled upon what I believed to be my true calling.

I'd been enjoying one of my lengthy periods of leisure, after a supermarket had let me go due to my reluctance to lift heavy boxes of beer onto the higher shelves, when an overbearing chap at the Job Centre told me to stop making excuses and start applying for at least a dozen jobs a week.

"Or else," he growled.

"Or else what?"

"Or else I'll have your money stopped."

I suppressed a smile, because I'd been threatened in this way before and my Contingency Fund meant that I could easily get by without the dole until I found my next job. I'd always rented, you see – people of my disposition rarely purchase a property – and I knew he couldn't touch my housing benefit, no matter how much I defied him. In the past, indiscriminate job applications had landed me in a foul-smelling canning factory (for five weeks), a funeral parlour (for three), and a slaughterhouse (for about four hours), so I wasn't about to risk my mental wellbeing just to toe this balding beggar's line.

By then, however, after at least fifteen spells on the dole since the age of eighteen, I preferred not to rock the boat if I could help it. Besides, a fun way to meet his quota had just occurred to me.

I grasped the little booklet in which I was supposed to note my applications and held it close to his beady eyes.

"I'll have a dozen for you next time, John."

"*Two* dozen, two weeks from now... Richie."

"Even better," I muttered, before signing on the dotted line, grinning at the miserable git, and loping out of the accursed place.

The February weather was foul, so I hunkered down in my cosy flat and got to work. Partly to annoy my persecutor, but mostly for kicks, I began to apply for an eclectic selection of posts, regardless of the requirements stipulated in the job descriptions. After dashing one off for a quantity surveyor position in Lancaster, I expressed interest in becoming a vet in Keighley and a mental nurse in Bolton. Closer to home I solicited the posts of solicitor in Accrington, imam at a mosque in Blackburn, and something called Operational Data Lead at Burnley General Hospital. There were several more that I don't recall now, but I believe the very last application of this kind was for the role of librarian in the small East Lancashire town which my dear sister has asked me not to name, her being on the council there and pleased to have the black sheep of the family over a thousand miles away, although she does visit me from time to time.

Most of these absurd missives were ignored, or course, as in most cases I'd simply skipped the lengthy application form in favour of a direct appeal to my prospective employer, but I did receive a rude email from the solicitor's, a ruder call from a rabid vet and, crucially, a personal visit from the local librarian.

By the time I opened the downstairs door I'd prepared an apology for the person whose job I presumed I'd applied for in such a foolish way, because of course I didn't have a single librarianship qualification to my name.

"Hello, Richie?" enquired a plump, smiling young lady.

"Yes, er..."

"Denise."

I pressed her proffered hand. "Well, er..."

"I was just passing and decided to ring your buzzer on the off chance."

I rocked from foot to foot with a sheepish smile on my face. I'd rarely visited the poorly stocked library since internet sellers had enabled me to buy cheap second-hand books with ease, but I perceived intelligence and amiability in her pleasant features and hoped that after my forthcoming apology I might be able to steer the conversation in a more agreeable direction. Then I recalled that her post was up for grabs, so she'd presumably be off to run a grander establishment elsewhere.

I followed up my frown with the confession that I wasn't a librarian and never had been.

"I know."

"So I'm sorry about my silly appli... what?"

"You applied for the post of library assistant."

"Did I... that's to say, yes, I did... didn't I?"

She sighed and shook her head sympathetically. "Ah, I know what it's like to look for work these days. We help people to do it at the library. You have to apply for *so* many jobs that you end up forgetting what the heck they were."

I readily agreed, then decided against raising a laugh by mentioning the other posts I'd so childishly put myself forward for. "Yes, library assistant, of course, now I remember."

She smiled. "Anyway, I just wanted to say that I.... we're going to invite you to an interview." She looked along the street of mostly terraced houses. "You can almost see the library from here."

I rubbed my hands together and nodded eagerly, having always hated commuting. My humble lifestyle made it inadvisable to run a car, although I had owned a couple in the past, and by then I was heartily sick of lengthy bus journeys and, worse still, expensive taxis after finishing a shift in the dead of night.

"Yes, it'd be the perfect job for me. I'm a great reader, you see," I said truthfully. "And I'm always keen to encourage others to read," I fibbed whitely.

She chuckled. "One of your... if you get the job, one of your tasks will be to get the youngsters off the computers and among the bookshelves... if you want to, that is."

"Oh, definitely." I pictured some of the more loathsome local youths leafing through slim volumes of Shakespeare's sonnets or immersed in great tomes like War and Peace.
"Yes, I'll... I'd do my best to promote the reading of good literature."
She sighed. "Even best-sellers would be a start. Anything to get them off their phones and tablets."
"Quite." I was just about to invite her for a coffee in a nearby cafe when I spotted her wedding ring. Job first, friendship later, I decided, before asking her when she wanted me to present myself.
"Tomorrow at two, if that all right with you."
I could almost feel my brown eyes gleaming with enthusiasm as I looked down the street towards the first workplace I truly wished to enter since narrowly failing to land a cushy administrative number at the Job Centre – such are life's ironies – many years earlier.
"That's perfect, Denise. Thanks ever so much."
I think I made to straighten an imaginary tie, because she told me to dress as I would on the job, before patting my arm and strolling back to the book-lined, computer-infested sanctuary which I so wished to share with her. I'll cater to her every whim, I swore as I bounded up the stairs, and stay there for a long, long time to come…

Despite being one O-Level short of the stipulated number, I made such a good impression on Denise and her two mature companions that I felt sure I had the job in the bag as I smiled one last time and closed the door quietly behind me. I was already an old hand at interviews, having had dozens of them over the years, and I believed I'd achieved such a guileful blend of gravity, cordiality and humility that the other lacklustre-looking candidates didn't have much of a chance. The fact that Denise and I liked each other would clinch it, I thought as I found myself approaching the door of the nearest pub, before performing a swift quarter turn and heading to the cafe for a celebratory cappuccino.

My failure to prosper in the world of work wasn't only due to my idleness, you see, because the Demon Drink had also scuppered more than one worthwhile opportunity. In my teens and early twenties, typical binge drinking had caused weekly hangovers and many an absence, leading to the sack on three occasions, once from a promising job at a plumbing supplies store where I was the apple of the owner's eye until I turned up late one Monday morning with two black ones and swollen knuckles to show that I might have given as good as I'd got. Much as the avuncular fellow admired his lanky protegee's pluck, he pointed out that a local business couldn't have its employees scrapping with potential customers, so he gave me a few sage words of advice and my P45.

Most young men ease off the binge drinking as they settle down and begin to raise a family, but I'd played the field with the local lasses so much, and achieved so little in life, that the shrewder damsels in my town proved impervious to my charms and ending up marrying more aspirational chaps. So it was that as I approached the end of my twenties I began to hit the booze in a more assiduous manner, sometimes spending whole weekends in the pubs, getting quietly sozzled as I watched soccer matches that didn't interest me and engaged in desultory conversations with the other local lushes.

This went on for at least half a decade, until one fateful day my father was diagnosed with cancer and given only months to live. He soon sold his prosperous roofing business and took to his bed, lamenting that my fear of heights had prevented me from following in his footsteps up and down the ladders.

"Yes, it's a shame that," I said on a sweltering summer Sunday afternoon in his darkened room.

"Though you should have gone to university really."

"Hmm."

"But in the end you've done neither one thing nor the other."

"No, Dad. The job at the petrol station is going OK though."

He sat up and glared at me. "Pah, petrol station! A brainless bloody moron could stand behind that till."

"They do. Take it easy, Dad."

He sniffed as I lowered his head to the pillow. "And you stink of booze."

"Sorry."

"Christ, who'd have thought you'd turn out to be the laughing stock of the town."

"Am I?"

"Course you are. Everyone likes to see their betters do badly. You should have left this dump at eighteen and never looked back. Either that or have built up the business all over

Lancashire, but you've done nowt worthwhile. Give me two of them tablets."

As he washed down the painkillers I felt a strong urge to get back to the pub and numb my sense of guilt with a few more pints, but in the event I walked straight home and went to bed. That week at work I suffered cold sweats, hot flushes and a little shakiness. My colleagues diagnosed the usual hangovers, but I was in fact coming off the booze cold turkey. During the final weeks of my father's life, in one of his more lucid moments he opined that there was hope for me yet.

"Yes, I think so, Dad. I've been reading a lot and I'm thinking of going to university at some point, though I'll have to get a couple of A-Levels first," I said, as my single D grade in French wouldn't gain me admittance to even the humblest former polytechnic.

"Hmm, your mum'll help you out financially, but what will it lead to, Richie?"

I shrugged, unwilling to state that I wished to study English Literature purely for my own satisfaction. "I expect I'll end up teaching."

"And do you want to do that?"

Shrug. "I don't mind."

"Oh, God." He raised a hand and let it fall. "I'd clobber you if I had the strength. I should've given you a few more good hidings when you were a kid."

I smiled. "You didn't give me any that I can recall."

"More's the pity. Your granddad sent me up a ladder with a kick up the arse. Oh, Richard, you're so bloody… aimless."

Aimless Richard doesn't have the same ring to it as Idle Rich, but I'd better get back to the library, as nothing I did during the intervening five years would have impressed my father, though at least he died believing that I wasn't a lost cause. Going to college to do A-Levels seemed like such a bore that I just carried on reading widely and even penned a few execrable poems from time to time. In this way I gradually metamorphosised from a drunken laughing stock into an aloof and rather pompous figure who now thought himself a cut above everybody else due to the book learning that was failing to lift him out of his usual round of menial jobs. Skilled working men who had laughed at me in the pub now pointed mockingly at me through the cafe window as I sat immersed in some erudite tome, as I wasn't averse to flaunting my scholarly aspirations in public, though standing at the bus stop in my Asda jacket can only have enhanced my status as an eccentric misfit who had somehow lost his way in life.

That was all about to change, however, because soon after becoming Denise's faithful assistant I began to study for my Level Three Diploma in Libraries, Archives and Information Services, a qualification which every self-respecting library assistant ought to have. For a man who had read and even partly understood James Joyce's Ulysses and had positively enjoyed most of Dostoyevsky's work, this diploma didn't tax me unduly, so after a year or so at the library Denise encouraged me to study to become a bona fide librarian.

"Oh, I don't know about that," I said as we sipped coffee at our table behind the counter. "I'd need to get a degree first, then do the postgraduate course that you did."

"Well then? You've been going on about doing an English degree ever since we met."

I shrugged. "Yes, well, but don't forget the brace of A-Levels I'd need to get first."

"Oh, you can easily do English Lit and something else at college, and they're so easy to pass these days that you'll hardly need to go to the classes. You look doubtful, as usual, Richie. You don't want to be a library assistant forever, do you?"

I smiled. "Yes, that's exactly what I want to be, especially if you stay here for the next… twenty-odd years until I'm allowed to retire."

She tutted. "No chance of that, I'm afraid. The way things are going in the library system I'll have to move to a bigger one, if I don't want to find myself out of work one day."

I gulped. "Surely they'll never close this one. I mean, it's a town of almost twenty thousand people, after all."

"And how many of them come in regularly to take out books?"

"Er, well, there's old George, Malcolm, Sheila, Dorothy… and quite a few more."

She sniggered. "Exactly. We could name them all in a few minutes."

"Yes, but don't forget our motley crew of computer users. There's no shortage of those."

"Before you started they used to have to book a slot on them. Now there's usually at least one free. No, with internet deals and phone packages getting cheaper all the time, it won't be long before hardly anyone bothers to come. I wouldn't be surprised if librarians become like vicars a few years from now."

"What? Giving sermons and whatnot?"

She giggled. "No, but these days vicars are often assigned to two or three churches, due to the tiny congregations. I guess each church might have a curate, so if a similar thing happens, you could end up running this place, but without much of a pay rise."

I sipped my tepid coffee and sighed. "In that case, you encouraging me to become a librarian might be a bit misguided."

"We'll always exist, but few youngsters choose this career path nowadays, for obvious reasons. You'd be covering your back, if you do want to stay in this line of work till you retire."

"Oh, why can't things just stay the same?" I lamented. "I just want to come here, read my books, write my bits and pieces, and get out walking when it's fine. Is that too much to ask, Denise?"

"You'll get bored eventually, and you're probably due for a mid-life crisis at some point."

"Oh, I don't know. I've reached forty without a hitch, and if we're sat here ten years from now, that'll suit me just fine."

She tutted and shook her head. "After the eventful life that you've told me all about, you really do seem to be becoming set in your ways. I mean, don't you want to have a girlfriend?"

"Hmm, yes and no. Julie and me used to get on fairly well, and I must say I do miss the... physical pleasures of a relationship."

"Is Julie the pretty teacher who you hide from when she comes in occasionally?"

"That's her. She ended up pressuring me all the time though. If we were still together, she'd be saying the same as you about me becoming a librarian. My sister Cathy does it too." I pushed back my receding brown hair and sat with my head in my hands. "A new girlfriend would mean there'd be three of you urging me onwards and upwards, when all I want is to keep my feet on the ground and my head... wherever it chooses to wander."

"Nicely put, but tell me, Richie. Don't you think you like your job so much because it must be just about the cushiest number going?"

I glanced through my fingers at the empty library and grinned. "Of course I do." I patted her hand. "And I love working with you, so with my chequered past you shouldn't be surprised that I'm happy with my lot." I grabbed our mugs and stood up. "Washing up doesn't do itself, then I'll tidy up the history section."

"You do that." She yawned. "I'll have a look into how many new books we can get this month."

"Ten?"

"Don't be silly. Lancashire County Council isn't made of money. Maybe half a dozen, if we're lucky."

"Ask for all six volumes of Proust's In Search of Lost Time."

"Fat chance. George wants the latest Jack Reacher book, and Sheila's asked for a novel called Shades of Grey or something."

"That's practically pornographic, my mum tells me."

"Got to please our customers, Richie."

I eyed the ceiling and pressed my palms together. "God preserve this seat of learning from further desecration."

"Amen."

Despite my ongoing lack of ambition, during my library years I did improve my lifestyle in a few tangible ways. I bought my first car for a long time, mainly to enable me to go for long walks further afield, and a chance meeting one day led to me joining a rambling group based in nearby Rossendale. We went out every Sunday, whatever the weather, and as well as making a couple of new male pals I became involved with a sweet divorcee called Sarah who worked in a chemist's shop in Ramsbottom. As her ex-husband had custody of their two kids at the weekends, we were free to do our own thing, so I was soon driving off from work on Friday afternoons and returning to my flat on Sunday evenings. At holiday times we sometimes had the kids in tow, and although I got on with them well enough, I didn't wish to usurp their father's place by becoming a key figure in their lives.

Sarah, once our carefree honeymoon period was over, soon got down to the important business of attempting to organise my future life. This included – as I'd predicted – me becoming a real librarian and hopefully finding a post closer to her three-bedroom semi which I was repeatedly invited to move into. To cut a long and not overly relevant story short, after two largely enjoyable years she was bringing so much pressure to bear that I gradually began to extricate myself from the well-intentioned web she was weaving before I got stuck there for good. On finally perceiving my lack of commitment, at thirty-six she decided that she couldn't afford to waste any more time on a man who refused to be tamed, so one spring Saturday morning she packed all the things I had lying around and gave me my marching orders. After that I thought it best to give up the Sunday walks, but she soon told me I was missed and oughtn't to deny myself that pleasure just because we were no longer together. So I resumed my rambling and it wasn't long before Sarah began dating a stolid software developer called Colin who she eventually married, so it was just as well that I'd wasted no more of her valuable time.

After an enjoyable spell of bachelorhood, I'd just begun to see an apparently carefree lady of my own age who worked in pest control and had visited the library to tackle the mice that were nibbling our antiquated selection of children's books, when my world came crashing down around me, as the cliché goes. One wet Wednesday morning in August I arrived at work to see Denise perusing a letter at our table. As her face was a little blotchy and she was sniffling, I asked her if she'd caught a cold.

"I wish. Have a look at this."

I was about to take the letter when she withdrew her hand. "No, it's up to me to tell you. As part of the latest round of cuts, they're laying you off, three months from now. I'm really sorry, Richie." To back up her words, she promptly burst into tears.

In order to console her for her impending loss, I put on a brave face and tried to make light of the disaster. "Well, we suspected that something like this was on the cards, and I'm glad it's me instead of you," I said, as none of her applications for librarianships in larger libraries had been successful. "I'll soon find something else, and to be honest, having so little work to do was beginning to get me down."

She wiped her eyes with a tissue. "Liar."

"Yes, well, but a change will probably do me good. In fact I might have a little rest, then start looking for a similar job," I said, despite the fact that during over five years of helping others with their job searches, I'd rarely seen the post of library assistant advertised.

"You might have to relocate to do that."

The idea of giving up my reasonably priced council flat didn't appeal to me one bit, and I had no desire whatsoever to go out into the big wide world, especially to do a low-paid job that could be axed at the drop of a hat.

"Hmm, well, I have a car now, so I can work at a library anywhere in Lancashire."

She sniffled and shook her head. "I think it's a non-starter, Richie. If you'd become a librarian... well, to be honest I'm not sure that would have helped much either. Nobody cares about libraries any more, except in university cities, maybe." She sighed and pushed herself up. "I'll make some tea."

"OK, thanks."

While she was in our tiny kitchen I wandered around the place, perusing our mediocre selection of books without seeing a single title. It was slowly beginning to sink in that I'd soon be back where I'd been until Denise had rung my buzzer on that fateful March morning. In three months' time I'd be back on that odious old merry-go-round of tiresome jobs, impulsive resignations, bad blood at the dratted Job Centre, and repeat, until retirement or death put an end to my misery... and I was still only forty-six years old! Mind you, as the years passed things would only get tougher, as no-one wants a grizzled old grump waiting on customers or moaning about his real or imagined arthritis as he's forced to cart heavy loads around. So it was that I returned to our dear old cup-stained table in a far less sanguine state of mind.

"You don't think they'd let me work two or three days a week instead of getting shut of me altogether, do you?"

Denise sighed. "I doubt it, but I'll tell them I can't possibly do without you." We both gazed around the empty place. "But I wouldn't get your hopes up, if I were you."

"I won't."

She sipped her tea and smiled. "Listen, I've just had a really off-the-wall idea that probably won't appeal to you, but I'll tell you anyway."

"I'm all ears."

"It has to do with my dad."

"He's in Spain, isn't he?"

"Yes, in a place called Chipiona."

"Never heard of it."

"It's a pleasant little town on the south coast."

"Oh, on the Costa del Sol, I suppose," I said with a grimace, as Sarah had once dragged me to Fuengirola for a week and I hadn't enjoyed the hot, crowded place much, never having liked sunbathing and no longer being a beer guzzler.

"No, much further west. It's a touristy place in summer, but it's mostly Spaniards who holiday there. My dad says there are hardly any Brits in the town, but quite a few other foreigners from various countries."

"Has he learnt Spanish?"

"Hmm, I think he gets by. He sort of ended up there by accident, you see."

"How's that?"

Denise told me that her dad, on becoming a widower at the age of sixty-three, had struggled to come to terms with his loss and been unable get used to living alone in the big old house in a hamlet near Blackburn where he and his wife had brought up their four children, Denise being the youngest. On winding up his fading career as a photographer, he'd begun to consider retiring to sunnier climes. His initial choice had been the Algarve, where his best friend Bill had already put down roots, so when he flew out on his annual visit he intended to rent a modest property for the winter and take things from there.

"While he was there an American pal of Bill's suggested a visit to a big naval base in Spain where he'd been stationed about thirty years earlier. This guy thought he could get them in to have a look around, and as Bill's into ships it was an opportunity he didn't want to miss, so they drove about two hundred miles and stayed at a hotel in a nearby seaside town. In the event even the Yank wasn't allowed into the base, because he hadn't brought the right documents, so they went back to the town to kill some time, as they were booked into the hotel for another night."

She chuckled. "My dad liked the lively old streets and the lovely beaches, but he was particularly taken by the lighthouse, the tallest in Spain. Bill was all for him finding a place near his in Albufeira, but my old man wasn't all that keen on the lifestyle there, mostly hanging out with other British expats, so... well, he told us that in Chipiona he managed sneak off alone and wander around for a while. He jotted down the phone numbers on signs on the houses that he liked the look of, though he wasn't sure if they were for sale or rent, as he knew hardly a word of Spanish.

"Anyway, back in Portugal he kept those numbers to himself and spent the rest of his holiday making one excuse after another for not renting any of the properties that Bill showed him. They ended up falling out a bit and my dad realised that it wasn't such a good idea to live so close to his old pal after all. He thought that a more adventurous move might help him to snap out of his melancholy mood – he refused to call it depression – so once he got home he called the half dozen numbers he'd noted down. The house he'd liked best was a pinkish colour, so it should have been easy enough to identify, as most of them are white, but he didn't know which phone number was which and none of the estate agents he spoke to had a pink property on their books, so he concluded that the only number he couldn't get through to must be the one."

Denise sipped her tea and glanced around, but the library was as empty as ever, so she went on with the tale that was beginning to intrigue me.

"For a while he gave up on the pink house and tried to convince himself that the Algarve was the most practical place to go, but he kept thinking and even dreaming about the house and that huge lighthouse, so in the autumn he booked a flight to Seville, hired a car, and drove down to Chipiona. It was much quieter than in summer, and to his surprise he found that his dream house was actually more of an orangey colour. He put his mistake down to the cheap sunglasses he'd been wearing that day, a terrible blunder for a professional photographer to make, he admitted. The sign was still up and a local estate agent soon showed him around the spacious old place on a quiet street not far from the centre. It had been the holiday home of a family from Madrid, but I think the owners had died and their heirs couldn't be bothered to go, so Dad snapped it up for what he thought was a good price. It turned out not to be such a bargain, what with all the work he had to have done, but it's worth quite a bit more now that the economy's improving."

Despite this positive outcome, Denise's expression had become more preoccupied as she spoke.

"How long has he lived there?"

"Er... he's just turned seventy-two, so about seven years."

"And is he happy there now?"

"Hmm, well, he seems content enough, but we're a bit worried about the way things are going."

"What things?"

She tapped her forehead. "He's begun to act a little strangely lately. He's always been a creature of habit, but those habits appear to be changing and he isn't keeping us in the loop as much as he used to. For one thing, because it's so busy in Chipiona in summer – positively heaving in August when most Spaniards have their holidays – he's always come home for few weeks and spent some time with each of us, until this summer, that is, when he only stayed for ten days and seemed impatient to get back."

I smiled. "I feared you were going to tell me he was becoming senile, but do you know what it sounds like to me?"

"What?"

"That he's got himself a girlfriend."

Denise stroked her chin and pursed her lips. "Hmm, I don't think so. My brother Simon had a quick trip out last month and there was no mention of a woman in his life. In fact Dad met him in Seville and took him to visit Jerez and Cádiz, so he only stayed in Chipiona for a couple of nights, where Dad wined and dined him like never before, as if he didn't want him to spend much time in the house."

"This only backs up my theory. Maybe he's shacked up with a lady who you might not approve of."

"I see your point and you may be right, but I still believe it's something else. Everything about him seems a bit rum, Simon says, and he wants us to send someone out to stay with him."

"Oh, I don't…"

"We were thinking of one of our kids. Not my two, as they're still at school, but my sister Adele's daughter doesn't start university until next autumn, and my brother Paul's younger son has just graduated and is struggling to find a job. Neither of them seems too keen to go to live with their granddad though, so we thought about a cousin of ours whose wife keeps chucking him out, but… well, the point is that we'd like to keep it in the family, but failing that I think a trusted friend would do just as well. So what do you think, Richie?"

"Er… I'm not really sure what you have in mind."

"Well, first of all you'd go to visit him. You've a week off in September, so you could go then, all expenses paid, of course. I'm sure you'd enjoy yourself in Chipiona and my dad really is good company."

I sniggered. "He might whisk me off somewhere like he did with your brother. Sounds to me that he's got something going on at home that he wants to keep to himself, thus his much shorter summer break this year. Must be a woman, if you ask me, unless…"

"Unless what?"

"Well, sometimes people… deviate sexually as they get older, don't they?"

She gasped. "You mean a man? Oh, I very much doubt it. He's always been one for the ladies, though he swears that he remained faithful to Mum, even when he used to shoot off on photographic jobs all over the place."

"Couldn't the four of you just make regular trips out to keep an eye on him?"

"We all try to go at least once a year, but with one thing and another we don't always manage it." She sighed. "His change of behaviour is so... pronounced, that at the back of our minds is the fear that he might be starting to lose his marbles. If this is the case, Simon wants him to come back to England sooner rather than later. Simon will be paying most of your expenses, by the way, and your, er... wages, if you decide to go back to stay with him."

"Why Simon?"

"Because he's loaded. He's got a big car dealership in Bury and his wife runs her own catering business. The rest of us will chip in too, but the idea is that Dad won't know that his companion's being paid."

"Right, well, I'll go and sort those books and have a think about it."

She smiled encouragingly. "You do that."

Over in our pitiful history section, which hadn't received a new publication for over two years, I strove to put the bigger picture out of my mind and concentrate on the forthcoming holiday, my very last one from our beloved library. The rat-catching lady who I'd been seeing wanted to take me to her parents' place in Cheshire, but as I didn't foresee our relationship prospering far beyond the physical stage, I thought it unwise to get my feet under her folks' table. This would indicate a commitment that I didn't wish to make, so if I were forced to go to Spain on a mission of mercy, I'd be able to avoid that unappealing trip. Besides, whenever Denise had mentioned her dad in the past it had usually been with a smile on her face, so I had a feeling that I'd enjoy myself with a fellow who'd photographed everything from the Cruft's dog show to the conflict in Ulster and was said to have many an interesting tale to tell.

After chucking a soiled and severely annotated book about the Eastern Question into the bin, I returned to our table and told Denise that I'd be happy to go to visit her dad in September.

Her lovely blue eyes lit up. "Oh, great! And then—"

I'd raised my hand. "There's no point discussing what might happen after that until I've been." I pictured myself tramping through the wintery streets to the Job Centre. "I mean, I do like the idea of staying in Spain for longer, but I'll have to meet your dad first and see how we get on."

"Of course."

"And, well, I'm not too keen on the idea of being paid a wage… or not for long. A grown man like me should be able to find a way to make some money… after a while."

She smiled. "Do you speak any Spanish?"

"Just a bit, but I'll try to learn it. I still remember some of my French, so that might help."

"Oui, bien sûr. Look, if it works out and you do go to spend the winter there, you needn't feel guilty about the money you'll be getting. Simon really is wealthy, and to be honest he's a bit of a control freak, so if he's willing to finance your stay, all the better for you."

I frowned. "Will… would I have to report back to him then?"

She grinned. "No, I'll spare you that treat. Just keep me up to speed and I'll spread the word."

You can probably imagine that for a man of my ilk the idea of a lengthy, all-expenses-paid stay in Spain sounded like just the ticket to take my mind off the uncertain future I was facing. Due to the impecunious lifestyle I'd led for so many years, I'd spent few holidays abroad or anywhere else of interest, so Denise's tempting proposal seemed like the opportunity of a lifetime to leave Britain and immerse myself in a new language and culture. By then I'd read just about every English literary work of any importance from Chaucer to the present day, so I liked the idea of the fresh intellectual challenge which a sojourn in Spain would afford me.

That's what I told myself as I performed a few perfunctory tasks, but there's no way I would have resigned from the library to take up an insecure post of this kind. No, the truth was that the mere thought of going back to my old life filled me with such a sense of dread and loathing that I believe I'd have been willing to care for lepers in the Congo rather than return to the Job Centre to see John's beady eyes leering at me over his desk. Denise had told me quite a lot about her dad and I believed that my mission would only fail if he found my presence in his house annoying, because I was going to do my damnedest to get my feet under his table and avail myself of Denise's brother's generosity. Not for an indeterminate length of time, I told myself, but even if I studied hard, I'd surely need a few months to learn the language well enough to enable me to find a job and tell the wealthy car dealer that I no longer needed his support.

I licked my lips as I opened my lunch box, despite the boring sandwiches I'd prepared. As I munched I began to fantasise about my day-to-day life in the home of my dear colleague's father. We'd probably rise at about nine and have a leisurely breakfast at home, before taking a stroll along the promenade, as it's important for older people to do daily exercise in order to stay in good health for many years to come. After reading for a while in my spacious room, I'd call... must remember to ask Denise his name... and invite him to lunch at a seafront restaurant, where I'd insist upon paying, with his son's money, as a token of my gratitude for allowing me to be his companion. After he'd sipped a couple of glasses of wine, though I mustn't allow him to overindulge, he'd wax lyrical about his photography days, telling me many a riveting tale that I might be able to transform into fine literary creations, because in warmer climes and with time on my hands I felt sure that I'd stop procrastinating and finally get down to writing something worthwhile.

After lunch we'd stroll home for a much-needed siesta, before each doing our own thing until it was time for our aperitif at the quaint beachside bar which my vivid imagination had just conjured up, along with a colourful cocktail that I soon swapped for an ice-cold alcohol-free beer, having recalled that I didn't drink any more. Hmm, yes, in my new life I mustn't weaken and begin to tipple again, lest I overindulge and become the laughing stock of my adopted town...

"A penny for your thoughts, Richie."

"Eh? Oh, just thinking about what I'll have to do before I shoot off to Spain."

Denise grinned. "What will you say to your new girlfriend?"

I glanced over at the corner where the now defunct mice had once done their nocturnal nibbling. "I'll just have to tell her it's over between us. I don't think she's that taken with me anyway, so I won't waste any more of her time. My mum won't be too pleased about me going, as we enjoy our Sunday teas, but I'll buy her a decent phone so I can video call her. As for my flat, well, I'm loath to give it up, in case things don't work out, so I'd better keep paying the rent for the time being."

"Of course." She sighed. "Depending on how you find my dad, steps may be taken to convince him to come home."

My vision of our pleasant tête-à-têtes by the ocean was replaced by a far more irksome one of me stuck within four walls with a man descending the inexorable slope to mental oblivion. I shook my head to dispel this depressing image.

"But I spoke to him the other day and he seemed fine. I sometimes think Simon's stirring up a storm in a teacup, just because Dad's behaviour doesn't conform to how he'd like it to be. I'm sure you'll find him as hale and hearty as ever and you'll really enjoy your week there."

"Oh, I'd forgotten I was only going for a week."

She chuckled. "You've been plunged in thought ever since I put it to you, wondering how it'll be, no doubt."

"Yes."

"In the meantime, something's occurred to me. It doesn't make much sense for you to go out for a week and then come back to doss around in the library for another... five weeks, I think it is, until they let you go."

"So what do you propose? If I resigned I'd lose any redundancy payment I'll be entitled to, though I don't expect it'll be that much."

She smiled. "No, only around three thousand."

I began to salivate. "Really?"

"Yes, more or less. No, I think your best bet is to phone in ill towards the end of your holiday. Your boss will be very understanding, but you'll have to fly home to get a doctor's note at some point. That'll also enable us to meet up and have a chat about how things are going with Dad."

"Right."

"If it looks like you'll be staying on, Simon will probably want to meet you, so we could get that out of the way, then I'll do my best to keep him off your back."

"Right, so basically I can go to Spain with a view to staying, then just nip home once to get a doctor's note and whatnot."

"Maybe twice, if need be, but we... Simon'll pay for the flights."

I eyed her shrewdly. "Simon or all four of you? I don't mind being maintained by a wealthy man, but I wouldn't want to take the bread out of your children's mouths," I said, already thinking, I'm ashamed to admit, about the likelihood of a longer-term life in clover.

She shrugged. "Each according to our means, which means Simon won't expect too much from a humble employee like me, but don't worry about that."

"Hmm, but isn't it a bit unethical for me to skive off my final weeks here?"

"And isn't it more than a bit unethical for this bloody Tory government to be destroying the library system that should be seen as a basic human right?"

I quickly erased an image of the local youths spending hours gaming on the computers from my malleable mind. "Hmm, yes, if you put it like that, it doesn't seem so bad."

She smiled. "And you're off on a mission of mercy, after all."

"That's right."

"Sacrificing your career prospects to rush to an old man's side who may or may not require your undivided attention." She sniggered. "Simon ought to compensate you for the massive loss of earnings you're likely to suffer."

I wondered how much Job Seekers' Allowance had risen to since I'd last claimed it. "I'll be grateful for just enough to get by until I find my feet. Oh, what's your dad called?"

"Peter."

"Peter, right, and… well, who'll you tell him is coming to visit?"

"We haven't quite decided yet, but we're thinking along the lines of a family friend who has to flee the country for a while."

I gasped. "What?"

She smiled. "But nothing too dramatic. As it's you who'll be going, you'll be my friend and colleague, because you are, and you'll have had to clear off for a while because of… a woman who's hounding you, for instance. How does that sound?"

"Hmm, well, Gemma could easily murder me with all the chemical weapons at her disposal, though I've a feeling she'll take my departure with a pinch of strychnine."

"My dad needn't know that. I like to think I'm his favourite, so if you're sure you're up for it, I'll call him later and see how he feels about putting up a harassed pal of mine."

"What if he says no?"

"Then we'll know that something is seriously amiss, because he's the most hospitable man you can imagine. I believe that even if he does have a strange kind of woman in his life, as you've hypothesised, he'll still feel obliged to take you in after I've made an earnest plea on your behalf."

"OK, but don't lay it on too thick. Hey, why don't you just tell him what may well be the truth, once today's terrible news has sunk in?"

"What's that?"

"That the idea of returning to my former life has plunged me into a severe depression and I'm badly in need of a change of scene... somewhere sunny."

"Hmm, I guess the nearer we stick to the truth, the easier it'll be for you, though I think I'll throw the woman angle in too, as it'll make you seem like a more colourful character. Dad hasn't got much time for losers, you see, if their failure in life is of their own making. You losing your job will also come in handy, because the large redundancy payment I'll tell him you're receiving will explain how you're able to live there for a long time."

"All right." I smiled on recalling that my actual payoff would swell my bank balance to over fifteen grand, by far the largest Contingency Fund I'd ever possessed. I believe I'd been so thrifty because deep down I knew that my cushy number at the library was bound to end sooner or later, as Denise could easily run the place on her own.

She strolled down an aisle and soon plonked a book down in front of me. Out of habit I checked the publication date.

"1966. Looks like a first edition."

"Well, it's the only one we've got, and the Spanish language won't have changed all that much in fifty years."

"Thanks, I'll keep it here to dip into whenever I get a free moment."

"It won't take you long to finish it then."

"And I'll order some modern books and see what resources I can find online."

"Bravo."

I rubbed my page-hardened hands together. "This is going to be the beginning of a great adventure."

"I hope so, I really do."

So during the following weeks I wound up my affairs. I decided to keep the flat for the time being, but I sold my tatty old car, plus a few other belongings that I'd miss were I to return home, partly to pressure myself into making a go of it in Spain, even if my stay at Peter's proved to be short-lived. I'd already become an online Hispanophile and I now fully intended to embrace the real thing as if my life depended on it.

2 – An Unexpected Welcome

So, what with one thing and another, one rainy Thursday in late September I flew to Seville in a sombre but optimistic frame of mind. It had been whilst driving me to Manchester airport that my younger sister Cathy had made her Idle Rich jibe, and I spent much of my time in the air promising myself that I'd really try to achieve something worthwhile in Spain. I strove to see my stay with Denise's dad as merely the initial rung on a ladder to some sort of success, rather than an opportunity to laze around and get a sustained suntan for the first time in my life.

Idle Rich, Idle Rich… yes, if I lived up to this catchy moniker, I'd surely find myself back in the mire once my companionship duties ended, I mused as we flew over the green-brown plains of central Spain, before opening a modern Spanish grammar book and doing a couple of exercises. In a few short weeks I felt that I'd made giant strides towards learning the language, as I'd spent endless hours watching online tutorials and making copious notes. When I listened to normal Spanish I still understood very little, but I could construct many useful sentences and hoped to be able to communicate with the locals to some extent.

"To learn Castilian is the key to my... success," I murmured to myself in Spanish as the sprawling, sun-drenched city of Seville came into view, and I was soon inhaling the warm air of my promised or at least promising land. After picking up the small Seat hatchback that Denise had insisted I keep until my quick visit home to get a doctor's note, I took the southbound dual carriageway past endless ploughed and cultivated fields. The flat, open countryside felt immense compared to the green hills and cluttered valleys of East Lancashire, and for the first time I truly became aware that I was finally in a position to change my lacklustre life forever.

"Mustn't balls it up with Peter though," I muttered as I skirted Jerez de la Frontera and headed west along another quiet dual carriageway towards my destination. The agricultural landscape had hardly changed since leaving the airport, comprising mostly huge fields of cereals and a few plantations of olive trees, but as I neared Chipiona I began to see a number of large greenhouses in the smaller fields which to my untrained eyes appeared to host a greater variety of crops. On spotting a dusty, dusky group of men who had just finished work for the day, in my air-conditioned cocoon I smiled at the idea of Richie Bannister joining them to do a bit of honest toil, though when I wound down the window it occurred to me that it might get a tad hot within the canvas structure they'd just emerged from, as it was still pushing thirty degrees at six in the afternoon.

Before locating my future home I made for the seafront and passed a modern marina before feasting my eyes on a golden beach through a row of flourishing palm trees. Back inland a bit on a narrow one-way street, I caught a glimpse of the castle and then, past the only large apartment blocks I'd seen, I beheld the structure which had so taken Peter's fancy on his initial visit seven or eight years earlier. The famous Faro de Chipiona didn't look all that majestic from a distance, but as I approached the impeccable sandstone tower, its height of nearly seventy metres did provoke a feeling of awe, not least because the Romans had built the first lighthouse there, way back in 140BC, assuming the Phoenicians hadn't beaten them to it, as that capable maritime race had certainly traded along the coast.

After parking up to take a better look at the lighthouse that had led to one man's inspired decision to retire to this lovely town, it occurred to me to phone to give him fair warning of my arrival, rather than knocking on his door as Denise wished me to do, in order to surprise him in his natural habitat and be able to form an objective first impression. As she and her siblings were my paymasters, however, I elected not to disobey their order and promptly instructed the satnav to find his house. It sent me round the headland and along another pristine beach on which a few people were strolling, before I turned back into the town and began to look out for the famous orangey-pink house. I loved the mostly low-rise nature of the resort – for resort it was, if only in summer – and I was simply itching to meet my host and hopefully take a leisurely stroll along the seafront, before inviting him to dinner with my *own* money, the least I could do after fate and Denise had sent me to stay in such a marvellous place.

On spotting the angular detached house, I was able to park right outside on the quiet street and I spent some time gathering my thoughts. Most of the white blinds were down on this and the adjacent properties, presumably to keep out the still warm rays of sunlight, but they made the place feel very private. Peter's probably in there with his lover, I surmised, maybe an ex-flamenco dancer of gypsy stock whose existence he wishes to keep from his family, and here I am, a complete stranger, about to burst into his life with some cock and bull tale about a troublesome female who's made me scarper to the other end of Europe. A likely story, I muttered as I opened the heavy gate and crossed the narrow patio adorned with a number of potted plants and quite a few weeds between the tiles. I'll soon make myself useful and pull those up, I decided, before knocking on the door.

I heard no movement within, so I knocked a bit louder before stepping back to survey the unwelcoming façade. Having complied with my employers' wishes, I was about to phone Peter when I heard a squeak and looked up to see that one of the upstairs blinds had risen by an inch or two. Not wishing to stare into the man's bedroom, I turned away and pretended to inspect a somewhat shrivelled shrub. I then leant against the metal fence to enable the occupant of the room to get a good look at me, because by this time I assumed that Peter had become a hermit or the blind had been raised by someone else's hand, perchance that of his sultry mistress.

On hearing a creaking sound, I glanced up to see that a larger opening had now been made. Through it I saw the wide eyes of a young, very black and masculine-looking face, before the blind was quickly lowered and I grasped a railing to support my shaky legs. Who in God's name could that have been? Unwilling to speculate on the situation for a moment longer, I whipped out my phone and pressed Peter's mobile number, already feeling that my cosy berth was in jeopardy. It wasn't so much because Peter appeared to be hosting a young black fellow, because there could be any number of reasons for that, but this blind-twitching episode was exceedingly odd and might spell an immediate end to my Iberian dream, or at least force me to put my yet-to-be-formulated Plan B into practice.

After listening to a standard Spanish answerphone message, I hung up and began to write him a text. My face must have shown the anxiety I felt, because a deep chuckle preceded the pat on the shoulder I received from a slim, grey-haired, deeply tanned man on the other side the railings.

"Travelling can be stressful, I know," he said in a Lancashire accent tempered by a slightly alien twang.

"Peter?"

"That's me." He strode briskly into the patio. "And you must be Richie, my daughter's pal who's fleeing from the wrath of a woman, ha ha."

I smiled as we shook hands. "Something like that," I said, as I knew right away that I'd struggle to fib under the gaze of such lively and penetrating blue eyes.

He unlocked the door. "Grab your bags and come on in. I was expecting you tomorrow, but I got your room ready this morning, just in case."

"Thanks."

He smirked on seeing my huge rucksack and smaller travel bag, before ushering me into a large, modern kitchen-diner overlooking a verdant rear patio with high plastered walls. The familiar click of the kettle and rustle of teabags helped me to relax, while his brisk movements reassured me that Peter was no doddering old fool, but as fit and healthy a septuagenarian as I was likely to meet. The black face at the window still troubled me, but I decided not to avail him of my sighting, preferring to wait for the man to emerge from hiding or, failing that, for Peter to explain his presence.

After we'd exchanged the usual niceties he asked me bluntly how long I planned to stay. His smiling reaction to my abundant luggage had given me time to formulate a response that I hoped would ease any worries he had about being burdened by an unwanted guest.

"Well, I've come with the intention of settling in Spain, though not necessarily around here. I've really enjoyed working with your daughter Denise for the last few years, but that's over now and I'm reluctant to go back to the usual round of dead-end jobs."

He eyed me mischievously over the rim of his mug. "So what makes you think you'll be any better off in Spain?"

Reacting rapidly to this incisive comment, I blathered on for a while about my desire to immerse myself in a new language and culture after spending my whole life in the same dreary Lancashire town.

"I know it well. It's no worse than anywhere else, but I must say I was glad to get out of Blackburn and into the country. My work trips kept me from getting bored too, but after my wife died and I retired I simply had to have a change of scene."

"Yes, Denise told me."

His eyes narrowed. "I bet she's told you a lot of things, eh?"

"Well…"

"Egged on by that controlling son of mine who came to check up on me not long ago."

"Hmm."

He patted my hand, just like his daughter was wont to do. "The best thing you can do is get shut of any preconceived ideas you've come here with."

"Yes."

"And just get the most out of your stay, without concerning yourself too much about what I get up to."

"I'll try not to get under your feet."

"What are your political views?"

"Er, well, I'd say I'm on the left, broadly speaking, but I haven't always bothered to vote."

"Why not?"

"Well, ever since Tony Blair made his mark, Labour haven't seemed much better than the Tories to me."

"What about the far right?"

"What about them?"

"Never been tempted to go down that road? You know, back to Britain for the British and all that?"

"God, no. I've read plenty of history and I know what that sort of thing can lead to. Most of them are a bunch of thugs anyway," I said, hoping he wasn't about to reveal himself to be a born-again white supremacist.

"I'm glad you feel that way." He drummed his fingers on the table and bared his still strong teeth in an impish grin. "I guess I can introduce you to Oumar then."

I feigned surprise. "Oh, who's that?"

"The lad you were looking at a while ago."

"Ah, yes."

"He texted me to say that he thought my visitor had arrived. He's not allowed to open the door, you see."

I gulped. "Right."

"I have strict rules about that sort of thing."

I sipped my tea. "I see."

"These people have to know their place, after all," he said sternly, then pressed his lips together so tightly that I was almost sure he was having me on.

I decided to go with the flow and show him that I was a perceptive sort of chap with a subtle sense of humour.

"Quite right. Do you allow him out of the room at all?"

"Oh, yes, they normally have the run of the house."

My poker face almost fell. "The… they?"

"Yes, I generally only have one at a time, but I make them earn their keep." He made his sandals squeak on the tiled floor. "Mopped to perfection only this morning. Oumar's even offered to cook one of his mother's tasty recipes, which is unusual for a Senegalese man."

"Ah, do you only have Senegalese then?"

"Up to now, yes, though they might well send me a Mauritanian or a Malian at some point."

"Uh-huh."

"Same neck of the woods, you see."

"Yes. I believe they all speak French, as well as their native tongues, of course."

He smiled. "That's right. In fact my main role, apart from keeping them off the streets and supplying them with certain things, is to teach them some basic Spanish phrases. An unusual task for a lousy linguist like me."

Having realised what he was up to, I asked him how long they normally stayed for.

"That depends on their connections. Sometimes just a couple of nights, but longer if they struggle to get in touch with the right people."

"I see."

"They've made it so far, so it's a shame when they get caught before they reach the relative safety of their community."

"Where's that?"

"Madrid or Barcelona is often their final destination, though they go to other cities too. Some try to make it all the way to France. It all depends on where their relatives or friends have ended up."

"I see."

He smiled. "So have you cottoned on to what I've been doing for the last few months?"

"I think so. Is it very profitable?"

He studied my impassive face. "Ha, now you're having *me* on."

"Yep."

He sighed. "They've spent enough by the time they reach here, often running up debts that take them ages to pay off before they can really begin to help the folks back home. It's something I got into quite by chance, but I enjoy it and I am actually hoping to be rewarded one day soon."

"Oh?"

"Yes, by accepting one or more of the invitations to Senegal that I've already had. I plan to fly from Madrid to Dakar and spend at least a month there, meeting some of the families of the blokes I've got to know."

"Wow, that'll be quite an adventure."

He shrugged. "A walk in the park compared to what my guests go through."

"So this explains your short visit home this summer."

He nodded, before telling me that until a retired teacher from the nearby town of Sanlúcar de Barrameda had got him involved in this benevolent people-smuggling caper, he'd preferred to clear off for most of July and August, because at the height of the holiday season the population of Chipiona swells from about eighteen thousand to nearer eighty, most of them noisy Sevillians who swarm all over the beaches, bars and restaurants. This year by July he'd become a key player in the network that enabled the migrants to make it from the beaches between Chipiona and Rota to Seville and beyond, so he'd been loath to shoot off at such an important time, when the small boats had their best chance of arriving from the west coast of Morocco, a distance of at least sixty nautical miles.

"Isn't it easier for them to cross near the Straits of Gibraltar?"

"Shorter, but far more dangerous, and the Straits are swarming with patrol boats and aircraft. This route is a relatively new one which the authorities didn't expect due to the big naval base being so close by, but the Americans there don't concern themselves with the poor folk fleeing Africa."

"Isn't it a Spanish base too?"

"Oh, they often have a couple of old frigates there and they're nominally in charge, but it's essentially an American base. They cosied up to Franco in the fifties and got it in return for lots of economic aid and a tacit agreement not to oppose the dictatorship. It's still strategically important, as it's a good stop-off point on the way to the Middle East, so there are still a few thousand Yanks living there."

I smiled. "You almost got in to see it once."

"Ah, yes, and if I had I wouldn't have been able to wander around this town and find my new home, so I'm grateful for their tight security. Anyway, since the spring quite a few pateras have been landing nearby, so until SEMAR increase their patrols to make it unviable, I'll be doing my bit to help those people to get where they want to go."

"What's SEMAR?"

"El Servicio Marítimo de la Guardia Civil," he said in what sounded to me like a good Spanish accent. "It's a long coastline and they only have limited resources, so up to now we haven't seen any more patrols than usual, but it'll only need some political bigwig to kick up a fuss for them to start speeding up and down till they've intercepted a couple of boats. Then the Moroccan people smugglers will find a new route, and so it goes on."

"What happens when a boat gets caught?"

"The smugglers get chucked in jail and the migrants are taken to a detention centre, usually the one in Tarifa, the windy surfers' paradise that you may have heard of."

"Yes. What then?"

"Well, they can only keep them there for sixty days, so if they haven't got round to repatriating them, they have to let them go, though sometimes it gets so overcrowded that they release them sooner. By then they've made contact with their people and can catch a bus to Madrid or wherever, but once there they have to be careful not to get nabbed again."

He went on to tell me that of the estimated 100,000 Senegalese in Spain, just over half had residence permits and about a quarter were fully fledged taxpayers. Unlike the British, most of them had no particular interest in living in Spain, as the fairly benign tropical climate of their own country afforded them plenty of sunshine. Often their aim was to make enough money to purchase land back home on which to support their families, but to do that they had to work like dogs in pitifully low-paid jobs.

"Only the ones who manage to get residency can aspire to earn the same as a Spaniard. For most the pinnacle of achievement is to get a council job. A guest of mine called Cheikh shed tears on telling me about his brother who'd become a dustbin man in Tarragona."

"Oh."

"Yes, he was so happy for him. Cheikh's ambition is to stand shoulder to shoulder with him on the bins, but he knows he oughtn't to get his hopes up too much, as dream jobs like that don't come up very often."

"No. I had a trial on the bins in Burnley once, but it was too hard for me."

"Nay, lad, binmen these days don't know they're born," he said in broad Lancastrian.

"They're an uncouth lot and they swore at me for going too slow."

He laughed and patted my hand. "You poor thing. Joking aside, getting to know these Africans really makes you appreciate the easy life we have. It puts all our trivial problems into perspective. Whenever I eat a bit of seafood with a glass of wine by the sea I'm sure I savour it more than before, when I thought it was my God-given right to live the good life."

I licked my lips and nodded.

"But I afraid I won't be eating out till Oumar's gone on his way. If he's stuck here it doesn't seem fair, but there's plenty of food in the fridge."

"I wanted to invite you to dinner, but that can wait. What'll happen if you get caught helping these migrants?"

"Hmm, well, I might get a fine and a slap on the wrist like the Spaniards do, or if I fall into the wrong hands I could be expelled." He jerked his thumb towards the wall. "Those neighbours are from Seville and it's their holiday home. She's a doctor and she once gave me a complicit look when she saw me arrive with a weary black lad, but I became more careful after that, mainly because of the neighbours on the other side. The bloke's got a big moustache, you see."

"Right."

He smiled. "Yes, right. Men who sport tashes in Spain are usually right-wingers, don't ask me why. Him and his wife are from a town called Écija, to the east of Seville, and they've been coming down a lot since they retired last year. They're not very friendly and when I've tried to strike up a conversation in my awful Spanish I've only had one-word answers, so I think they're down on foreigners in general. If they see one of my African guests, I've a feeling they'll go squawking to the Civil Guard, so when they're here I'm extra careful. More often than not I fetch guests to the house in the dead of night, and more than once I've had to get them out the same way, but I guess it's all good fun."

"Fun?"

"Oh, it adds a bit of spice to an otherwise unexciting life. There's only so much sunshine a man can stand, and after a few hundred dips in the sea even that becomes a bit tedious. Anyway, as the neighbours' front blinds are normally down, I tend to leave mine down too, so my guests can have the run of the house." He glanced up. "It looks like Oumar's skulking in his room. He's a shy sort of lad and he mustn't have liked the look of you."

"Oh, shall I clear off for a bit then?"

By way of reply he fetched a keyring from a drawer and handed it to me. "You're free to come and go whenever you want."

"Thanks. I'll go for a stroll later, but I'd quite like to meet Oumar first."

"Why?" he said in that direct way of his that I believed was intended to elicit an honest response.

I smiled. "Why not? I've never met anyone from Senegal before, and it'll give me food for thought when I go for a wander."

"Do you think what I'm doing is wrong?"

I pondered for a while before attempting to answer this ticklish question, then told him that I thought it was undoubtedly a humane thing to do, although it would be better to regularise the immigration process and invite people to come to do the available jobs. His response surprised me.

"Ah, yes, in an ideal world that would happen, but it isn't, so it doesn't. You know, the good thing about these Senegalese blokes is that they come here to make money and aren't intent on bringing the whole family with them, as often happens with immigrants to Britain, thus making them a burden rather than an asset. I know that's not a very politically correct thing to say these days, but Spaniards don't mince their words about these matters like we tend to do, saying one thing but thinking something quite different. Do you agree, Richie?"

"I… I think so."

"You sound doubtful. Look, if a Polish guy goes to England to graft in a factory where our unemployed are too lazy to work, he's an asset, but if he brings his wife and kids he becomes a liability, as their schooling costs a lot more than what he contributes in taxes. I'm not saying they don't have a right to do that, but economically speaking it makes no sense."

"Hmm, I guess that's crossed my mind too."

"Right, well that's the way I thought about immigration until I got into this lark, and my views haven't changed altogether, but when I started to meet these men who're desperate to better themselves and their families, my stance began to soften." He smiled. "What I'm trying to say is that

I'm not some woolly Guardian reader who can't see both sides of an argument. No country wants to be flooded with a load of foreign folk who're just after what they can get." He pointed at the ceiling. "But when I think about that shy lad up there and what he might achieve after a few years in Spain, well, my heart goes out to him and I'll do whatever I can to help."

This earnest speech made the blood rise to my face, then he surprised me yet again.

"It might be best if you go out to have a look around now, after you've freshened up, of course."

"Oh, OK."

"Take your time and grab a bite to eat. It'll give me chance to convince Oumar that you're one of the good guys, though that's not the main reason. I realise you haven't come here to get involved in a strange business like this and you're going to have it on the brain as it is. Go out and get a feel for the place on your own. I think Oumar will be gone in a day or two, then I'll have time to show you around before the next one comes. In winter we don't expect many boats to arrive, and to tell you the truth I'll be ready for a rest. You'll find a clean towel in the little bathroom just there. I'll take your bags up in a while."

"Thanks."

After I'd spruced myself up, I asked him to recommend a good place to eat.

He smiled. "All in good time. On your first evening in your new country you ought to fend for yourself. There's just one thing I don't want you to do."

"What's that?"

"Don't bring a bird back to stay."

"Oh…"

"Any other time'll be fine, but not tonight, for obvious reasons."

"Especially if she has a moustache," I quipped, before he escorted me to the door and gave me an encouraging pat on back.

"And try not to get too drunk, Richie."

"There's no danger of that."

Peter was right about me having his clandestine caper on the brain, because as I made my way through the quiet streets to the seafront I could think of little else. Although I was impressed by the selfless commitment he'd made, I was glad that he didn't host these brave people all the time, and his mention of a winter hiatus had come as something of a relief. I was Idle Rich, remember, so anything that smacked of going the extra mile was still alien to me.

In the fading light I walked past an impressive church that was lit up like a Christmas tree and I realised that it must be the Santuario de Nuestra Señora de Regla de Chipiona that I'd read about. Rebuilt in 1906 in the Neo-Gothic style, it's still run by the Franciscan order and… and as I write I yawn at the prospect of describing all the old buildings I've come across up to press, so I decide on the spot not to bother unless it's something that particularly tickles my fancy.

Chipiona's castle, for instance, is nothing to write home or anywhere else about, and it was used as a prison and a hotel before the town council bought it and tarted it up for the tourists. It does house what they call the Cádiz and the

New World Interpretation Centre, which tells you all about the part the province played in the initial voyages to America. It's worth a visit on a rainy or especially windy day, because the one downside of what's been christened the Costa de la Luz – the Atlantic coast from Tarifa to the Portuguese border – are the constant and sometimes extremely strong winds which made the arrival of the flimsy pateras all the more remarkable.

Anyway, that evening I strolled along the pristine beach as far as the lighthouse that was so brightly lit that the revolving beacon itself seemed scarcely necessary. I then reluctantly left the promenade to seek out an unprepossessing bar in which to lose my linguistic cherry, as apart from saying adios to the English-speaking car rental man, I had yet to try out my Spanish on anyone other than a pretty Valencian girl on a YouTube channel who of course couldn't hear me. During my weeks of online research I'd often come across a common problem that aspiring linguists face when they attempt to strut their stuff on the Spanish coast, that of being replied to in English by the workers who are programmed to receive only monolingual Brits. In this respect I'd say that the Costa de la Luz is a great place to go, because the tourists are mainly Spaniards, apart from a few discerning foreigners who are willing to tax their brains sufficiently to at least open a phrase book and give it a go.

After passing a couple of large, brightly lit restaurants with few customers, I stumbled upon the Bar Peña Bética de Chipiona, ostensibly run by and for fans of Seville's Betis football club and occupied by about a dozen blokes watching a match on TV. My angular and distinctly un-Spanish face elicited no interest from the punters up at the bar, and after I'd sat down at a table by the window a plump young waiter bustled over, pad in hand.

"Good evening, I would like to eat," I said in Spanish.

"Muy bien, tenemos…" and he proceeded to reel off an unintelligible list of dishes about three times as fast as my lovely Valencian youtuber usually spoke, and much less clearly, because his lispy accent was barely decipherable to my untrained ears.

"Un momento," I said as I coolly raised the menu to my eyes.

"Para beber?"

"Oh, cerveza… sin alcohol, por favor."

"Muy bien." He trotted off.

I recognised many of the items on the menu due to my intensive study of food vocabulary, but unfortunately I couldn't remember which was which, so I'd just decided on a mixed fish platter when he plonked something looking very much like it in front of me. Believing that the efficient lad had read my mind, I asked him what it was.

"Tortillitas de camarones. Nuestra especialidad."

"Gracias. A mixed fish platter too, por favor."

He smiled for the first time and pointed at the batter covering whatever it was that he'd given me. "Mucho colesterol, no?"

"Oh, is the mixed fish platter… similar?"

"Rebozado, sí," he said, presumably meaning battered. "I can recommend our homemade meatballs in sauce, with chips," he pronounced more slowly. "Para acompañar los camarones, er… how you say… shrimps."

Fearing that the floodgates of his English were about to open, I promptly accepted his suggestion and began to tuck into the delicious battered shrimps, but I needn't have worried, because all our snippets of conversation from then on were in Spanish. As he'd identified me as a rudimentary linguist, he took pains to enunciate his words more clearly, as if speaking to a partially deaf or mentally challenged person.

"A little red wine with the meatballs?" was a suggestion I almost acquiesced to out of politeness, but I was wise enough to decline, knowing that the odd glass of wine might lead to more frequent indulgence and turn me into a booze-befuddled barfly, a surefire way of ending up back in Lancashire without a penny to my name. Peter's nose was as brown as the rest of his well-preserved face and I felt sure that he wasn't a heavy drinker, so whenever he partook of a glass of beer or wine I'd just have to remind myself of the bad old days and remain as dry as I'd been since then.

"Do you know Peter?" I asked the waiter when he brought my black coffee.

"El Inglés? Of course, everybody knows Peter."

"I am his friend. I stay with him in his house."

"How nice for you. He is an agreeable man." His face seemed to cloud over momentarily. "Sí, a very agreeable man."

As I couldn't remember how to say, 'what were you going to say?', I couldn't say it, so instead I asked him the first thing that popped into my head.

"Does he have many friends in the town?"

"Oh, yes, he knows a lot of people. Are you... alone with him in the house now?"

"Sí," I said without hesitation, now regretting that I'd mentioned my host, for although the young chap didn't have a moustache, who was to say if he or the people he knew were opposed to the underground activities that he might or might not suspect Peter of being involved in?

Not wishing to clamp up after his apparently pointed question, I asked him the next thing that popped into my head.

"Does Peter come here often?"

The lad seemed to sigh silently. "He used to come." He glanced towards the bar. "And I hope he will come again, when he... wants to."

"Muy bien. La cuenta, por favor."

"Right away."

My eyes followed him back to the bar and I noticed at least three moustachioed soccer viewers, but the gossipy murmuring I feared didn't occur and he came straight back with the very reasonable bill.

"Los camerones... the shrimps... invita la casa," he said.

"Oh, muchas gracias."

"De nada. We hope you will return."

"Yes, I will return soon."

After leaving a decent tip I took my leave and strode out and around the corner, before peering in through a small side window, half expecting the waiter to be huddled with a couple of the customers, reporting on Peter's European guest, but the lad was leaning on the bar, looking at his phone, so I walked away believing that I'd been reading too much into his clouded brow and ambiguous comments.

As it was still quite early I returned to the seafront and stepped onto the beach, now much narrower due to the incoming tide. Instead of cheerfully inhaling the salty air and looking forward to my immersion in Spanish life, as I'd expected to do, I found myself picturing the arrival of a patera. The smugglers would avoid the town, of course, and instead steer their human cargo towards a deserted stretch of beach, where they'd drop them off in the shallow water before speeding back to Morocco with their pockets full of money.

What then? I wondered as I strolled along by the shore. Would Peter and his companions be there to meet them, or would the exhausted travellers hide somewhere inland before making contact on the mobile phones they presumably possessed? These questions and others occupied my mind as I made my way towards the lighthouse which the smugglers surely used to situate themselves before veering off to a random or chosen spot on the ten-mile stretch of coast between Chipiona and Rota. I couldn't walk as far as the lighthouse, however, due to a rough stone structure that blocked my way, so I resolved to ask Peter about that when I got back and make no mention of my conversation in the bar.

As I zipped up my flimsy jacket against the now chilly breeze I had a sudden attack of cold feet regarding this whole immigrant business. Having expected to meet a carefree retiree enjoying his autumn years by the sea, I was in danger of getting embroiled in an illegal scheme to help a lot of folk who I didn't know from Adam. The old Richie had rarely lifted a finger to help anyone other than his family and the odd friend in need, so why on earth would I want to get myself mixed up in something that could result in me being plonked on a plane back to England, possibly after paying a massive fine that might obliterate my precious Contingency Fund?

As I gazed out to sea and up at the starlit sky I told myself not to get sucked into Peter's foolhardy enterprise. I'd be polite to his current guest, of course, but I'd make it clear to my host that I didn't wish to get involved. I'd come here to learn the language with a view to making a living sometime in the not-too-distant future, so all my mental and physical energy ought to be directed towards that end. On the way back to the house a dynamic plan occurred to me that I could put into effect if the stream of guests proved too distracting or stressful for me. There was nothing to stop me from taking off on an exploratory trip around southern Spain for a few weeks, improving my language skills and immersing myself in the historical and cultural wonders of Andalucía. By the time I returned, the worsening weather would have prevented all but the most reckless people smugglers from making the perilous journey, so my host might choose to raise the blinds and take it easy for a while.

No, there was nothing to stop me doing that, I thought as the conspicuous house came into view, except that I'd have to forfeit the wages paid to me for keeping an eye on a perfectly rational and healthy old fellow. I'd spoken briefly to his son Simon on the phone and that friendly but somewhat pushy man had insisted on me keeping his sister up to speed about every little thing that their old man got up to. As Denise and I were such good friends, under normal circumstances I'd have probably spilt the beans about her dad's daring exploits, but the last thing I wanted was for the meddling car dealer to kick up a fuss and possibly even order me to try to put a stop to his altruistic actions.

If I've rambled on about my tortuous thought processes, it's mainly to underline the mental turmoil I experienced during what ought to have been an enjoyable evening stroll. What a spineless, self-serving wimp, you're probably thinking, but if you put yourself in my place, you'll realise that for a lifelong shirker like me I had a heck of a lot of potentially irksome things on my mind.

Oh, this is a far cry from the delightfully sociable evening I'd envisaged, I thought as I inserted my front door key for the first time, and now I'll have to be polite but aloof so that Peter doesn't see the slightest collaborative gleam in my cowardly eyes.

3 – An Unexpected Reaction

I found Peter in his austerely furnished living room, sitting face to face with a dark, wiry lad of about twenty whose bloodshot eyes looked up at me fearfully.

"Calme, calme, Oumar. C'est mon ami, Richie. C'est un homme bon." He patted Oumar's hand, then pushed the armchair back and smiled at me. "I've been having to use my awful French on the lad."

"Très bien," I said fluently as I smiled benignly at the cowering chap.

"He's been fairly calm so far, but he was so tired and dehydrated when he arrived that all he felt was relief on finding himself here. Now he's starting to get the willies about what's in store for him."

"I know the feeling," I murmured.

"Sorry?"

"Oh, nothing." I approached the lad with my hand outstretched. "Er… enchanté, Oumar. Je suis Richie. Je suis… aussi nuevo… er, nouveau en Espagne."

Oumar pressed my hand softly and managed a feeble smile. "Encantado, Richie."

"He seems to know a bit of Spanish, so I'd like him to practise while he's here."

I found myself beaming. "Muy bien. Oumar, yo también hablo solo un *poco* de español. Tu y yo... hablar, practicar, sí?"

"Sí, sí... Richie."

Peter nodded approvingly. "Take a seat and I'll make some chamomile tea to help us unwind."

When I sat on the sofa beside Oumar he looked at me expectantly, so I wracked my brain for something uplifting to say. Asking him if he'd had a nice trip was a no-no, so I enquired after his family in Senegal.

He bared his fine teeth in a real smile. "Ma mam... mi madre... está bien."

I asked him if he had any brothers or sisters.

"Oh, sí, dos hermanas en Dakar. Un hermano en Dakar, y dos hermanos en España."

"Ah, dónde están?"

"Uno en Madrid. Uno en Zaragoza."

"Cómo se llaman?"

"Idrissa en Madrid. Moussa en Zaragoza."

"Qué... trabajar?" I said, my frail grammar having deserted me.

He smiled. "Moussa está en... comment dit-on? Où l'on fabrique des choses."

"Ah, en una fabrica," I said eagerly. "In English, a factory," I added irrelevantly.

"Sí, en una fabrica." He leant forward and tapped the coffee table. "Una fabrica de... des meubles."

"Muebles, sí, una fabrica de muebles."

"Oui, c'est ça. Una fabrica de muebles."

That's probably quite enough of our clumsy conversation for you to get the picture, so I'll spare you any more for the time being. After committing a slight faux pas by asking after his father, who seemed to have deserted them some years ago, I elected to concentrate on the brothers who lived in Spain. Through a mixture of Spanish, French and sign language I learnt that his brother Moussa had been settled in Zaragoza for about eighteen months. His employer was helping him to get his residence permit while paying him five euros an hour in cash, a figure that sounded low to me, but which Oumar assured me was quite good for a 'sin papeles' (a person without papers). He told me that Moussa shared a sixth floor flat with three of his countrymen, before scampering upstairs to get some photos just as Peter walked in with the tea tray.

"Frightened him off, have you?"

"No…"

He grinned. "I've been eavesdropping and you're doing a great job. I'll just do a bit of tidying up while he goes on with his life story."

"OK."

So Peter returned to the spotless kitchen while I viewed a few pictures of some smiling Senegalese men in what looked to me like a really crummy flat. Oumar told me they were content with their lot, as although only one of them had acquired the magical residence permit, they were all working and not being bothered by the authorities.

His brother Idrissa, on the other hand, was having a tougher time in Madrid. It sounded like he was sofa-surfing in the central Lavapiés neighbourhood where hundreds of his compatriots also lived. Although he'd been there for three years, he'd never had a regular job, instead having to hawk cheap watches, jewellery, knockoff designer clothing and the like, which he'd place on a blanket that he had to swiftly fold up and grab whenever the cops were spotted. The goods were supplied by documented countrymen who drove modern vans, so I suspected it was a well-organised network which offered the participants little chance to better themselves. Idrissa did manage to send some money home, but he was becoming disheartened and inclined to throw in the towel and go back to Dakar to buy a share in a traditional fishing boat.

The youngest brother, Modou, was at college in Dakar, funded by Moussa and Idrissa, and aspired to become a doctor, so in a sense their hopes were pinned on the bright nineteen-year-old, though there was still a long row to hoe, for all four brothers, before he'd be able to don a white jacket and stethoscope and earn some serious money… in Europe, of course, as doctors in Senegal earn a pittance in comparison. Oumar intended to do his bit to fund his brother's education, and while talking about his family's aspirations he became quite animated, although he didn't have much to say about his two younger sisters, other than that he hoped they'd manage to marry well.

By the time Peter came in to partake of some cool chamomile tea, Oumar was telling me that although he'd prefer to go straight to Zaragoza, he felt obliged to first look up Idrissa in Madrid. Using simple words and some creative gesturing, I strove to convey that he ought to make his stay in the capital a short one, before jumping on a northbound bus to join Moussa in Zaragoza.

"This is better, yes," he said in Spanish. "But depend what Idrissa say."

Then the lily-livered man who back on the beach had been conniving to stay well away from these needy Africans patted his jacket pocket and rubbed a finger and thumb together.

"Madrid to Zaragoza, I pay, OK? Not a problem."

"Gracias, Richie, but I have money… gracias," Oumar said before yawning mightily and covering his mouth. "Perdona, j'ai sommeil… cansado."

Peter grinned at me. "Don't worry, we've got a fund for that sort of thing," he said rapidly in English. "Let's get him to bed while he's cheerful, then he might have sweeter dreams."

So we soon bade the smiling lad goodnight and settled back to reflect for a while, because Peter seemed no more inclined to talk than I did. My thoughts revolved around Oumar's future in Spain and I pictured him on a Madrid-bound bus, wondering how his new life was going to pan out.

When Peter judged that my period of pondering was coming to an end, he said he wished to hazard a guess as to what my final thoughts were.

"Go on then."

"You're wondering if I ever suggest staying here in Chipiona to any of them."

"Wow, yes, how did you know that?"

He shrugged. "A few of us have proposed housing someone we particularly like, but our group's policy is not to do that."

"Why not?"

"Think about it. If Oumar were to stay here, it'd draw attention to what I'm doing. I bet the suspected Francoists next door would be on to the authorities like a shot, and even if the police didn't do anything, it'd prevent me from going on with my work."

"He could live somewhere else."

He smiled. "Rent's not cheap in a place like this. Besides, there are a few Senegalese living just up the road in Sanlúcar. Guess how they make a living."

I recalled the dusty, dusky workers I'd driven past a few hours earlier, though it seemed like an age ago. "Er, working in those big greenhouses?"

"The employers prefer Moroccans, as most of them have their papers. Try again."

"Er... oh, selling stuff on a blanket, I suppose."

"That's right, just like Oumar's brother in Madrid. I believe they do all right in summer, unless the cops confiscate their goods, but the locals haven't got much time for them, so... well, for all those reasons we don't host any of them for more than a few days." He smiled. "It's long enough to get attached though. I've stayed in touch with four lads and it'll hopefully be their families I go to see when I fly to Dakar."

"Do any women come on the boats?"

"Only a few, maybe one in fifteen or twenty, but women or couples take them in, for obvious reasons."

"And kids?"

"None so far, thank God, though one lad who stayed with someone else was only sixteen, so he'll probably end up being deported if he gets picked up. Oumar's twenty-one."

"Yes, he told me."

Peter nodded and smiled. "I must say you two seemed to get on like a house on fire. He's been more reticent with me, maybe because I'm older and a bit serious looking. You drew him out in Spanish too. I hadn't realised how much he knew. Ha, I believe you're a born teacher, Richie."

I blushed modestly. "Oh, I don't know."

"Have you ever done any?"

"Any what?"

"Teaching."

"No." I cast my mind back over my lamentable working life. "I can't remember ever having taught anyone to do anything much, except showing a lad the ropes in a cafe once. Then they gave him my job because they could pay him less."

He sniggered. "Oh, poor Richie, it seems to me that you've been your own worst enemy."

Stung by his bluntness, and a bit piqued by the fact that he'd reached this conclusion after knowing me for only a few hours, I said that not everyone was lucky enough to have a vocation they could pursue. I pointed at a dramatic black and white landscape photograph on the wall.

"You've had your photography, after all."

He laughed. "That's not mine. It's a limited edition print by the great Ansel Adams. He had two vocations, music and photography, but in the end he chose the latter. As for me, well, I just drifted into it. My first photography job, if you can call it that, was doing a cousin's wedding with a borrowed camera when I was eighteen. They were pleased with the results, so I bought my own and began to tout for business. I did weddings, family portraits and other odd jobs till a bloke I'd met got me some work on the Lancashire Evening Telegraph. From there I went to the Manchester Evening News and with them I got to go on more interesting assignments. Eventually I went freelance and managed to keep the wolf from the door till I called it a day."

I smiled. "How was Cruft's?"

"Lousy, as the mutts wouldn't keep still, but good pay."

"And Northern Ireland."

"Lousy pay, as I went there on spec, but it was quite an experience and I did manage to sell a couple of pictures to the Guardian. In a way that month in Belfast reminds me of what I'm doing now."

"How's that?"

"Well, I was in a bit of a rut and that trip opened my eyes to a lot of things. Bloody religion was making those people's lives a misery and I realised how lucky I was to live in a safe place. After that, every time I got bored I'd shoot off somewhere a bit more… challenging. I went to Afghanistan during the Soviet occupation, and to Palestine three times in the nineties."

"So were you a sort of war photographer?"

"God, no, I tried to stay well away from any gunfire, though I did hear some in the West Bank. No, I was after human interest photos. I took a few decent ones, but my wife wasn't keen on me doing those trips."

"Too dangerous?"

"Partly, but I think it was more because I normally made a net loss." He smiled and shook his head. "My Malawi trip in 2002 really pissed her off. It cost me a fortune and the famine there barely made the news, so I didn't sell a single picture. That was my only real taste of Africa, because a cruise I did down the Nile for a mediocre travel magazine hardly counts. Anyway, throughout my life I've found that a walk on the wild side from time to time does me a power of good. Coming here without knowing a soul helped to buck me up after my Mary died so young, but as I said, everything pales after a while, so I was glad when this business came up." He yawned. "About time I hit the sack."

"Me too. You know, Peter, I think it's turned out to be my most exciting day for... God knows how long."

He punched me lightly on the knee. "And you ain't seen nothing yet."

Later in my comfy double bed I recalled how I'd decided not to get involved, but there'd be time enough to wriggle out of any plans Peter might have for me in the coming days. I'd been momentarily fired up by certain things before, but I guessed that in the end my idle nature would prevail... or would it?

4 – An Eventful Day

"Ouch," I said as the old fisherman stabbed a defenceless octopus in the shallow pool.
"The food chain can be brutal."
"Let's leave him to it."
"Hasta luego, Andrés," Peter hollered as we began to clamber down from the long stone structure on the beach that I'd enquired about over breakfast. Despite the howling wind, we'd left Oumar to get ready for the next stage of his journey and come to inspect the famous Corrales de Pesca – roughly translated as Fishing Enclosures – which I'd stumbled upon the previous evening.

Ever since Roman times, if not before, this ingenious fishing method has been used in several places along the Cádiz coast. Peter explained that when the tide comes in, the fish end up in the large pools which empty quite quickly as the tide recedes, due to a series of metal gratings that allow only the small fry to return to the ocean. Until the twentieth century many households made a living in the Corrales, but nowadays only a few mostly older men don their waders and come armed with their nets and sharp forks to catch fish and squirmy seafood for their own consumption, as it's illegal to sell anything caught in this time-honoured way. The roughly made walls were in danger of being washed away until a local association was founded in the 1990s, and all the members are expected to help to repair them after each storm.

"Have you had a go?" I asked him as we walked towards the lighthouse.

"Oh, Andrés and his pal Juan offered to show me the ropes, but I prefer just to watch. I have helped out with the repairs, as there's often a slap-up lunch afterwards, but… well, as an outsider I don't like to encroach too much, and it seems a bit cruel, being so close to the fish and running them through with the fork."

"I guess so."

"Where did you eat last night, by the way?"

Funnily enough, I'd just been thinking about the previous evening and had renewed my resolve not to mention how my imagination had run riot in the bar.

"Oh, I had a quick bite in the Betis supporters' bar, then wandered along the beach."

"I like that bar, but I haven't been for a while."

"Ah."

He chuckled. "Since I joined the walking group there are certain people I prefer to stay away from, and some of them are regulars there."

"The walking group?"

"Oh, did I not say? Yes, the organisation likes to call itself a walking group. It has no online presence or official meeting place or anything like that, but we refer to it as our walking group."

"Why's that?"

"Oh, it's the brainchild of Elise, a Belgian lady who started off on her own, then began to recruit other people."

"All foreigners?"

"No, about half and half. There are about twenty of us now and whenever we speak on the phone or write texts we pretend that we're arranging walks or mentioning walks we've done and so on."

"Sounds a bit strange."

"Well, maybe we're being overcautious, but we want to operate well below anybody's radar. Besides, it's fun to come up with good cryptic messages."

"Such as?"

"Oh, 'do you fancy a moonlit walk along the Punta de Candor beach later on?' someone might write, always in English, as everybody understands it well enough. 'Yes, I'll pick you up at one and we could walk for about two hours,' could be the reply, depending on the boat's estimated arrival time. Things like that."

"A lot of night walks then."

"Almost always, unless the smugglers time it wrong and get in after sunrise. Ha, we've had a couple of hairy escapades when that's happened, but it's turned out all right so far, touch wood."

"What are the smugglers like?" I asked him, having imagined a bunch of evil pirate-like figures who'd be apt to cut one's throat for a few silver pieces.

"Well, we rarely see them up close, but most of them look quite young. They're risking their lives too, just like the drug and tobacco smugglers do, and I doubt the people who pilot the boats make all that much money. It's the fat cats back in Tangier or wherever who'll be raking it in, just like in all organised crime."

"How do the migrants get from Senegal to Morocco?"

"On a boat up the coast if they can afford it, or hitchhiking through Mauritania if they can't. I think Oumar took a bus from Dakar to Nouakchott, then a boat to Agadir, then more buses to a small town just south of Tangier."

"And how much does the boat trip to Spain cost?"

"I don't ask, but I think it's somewhere between one and two thousand euros, a vast amount of money for them. It's cheaper to get to the Canary Islands, particularly Fuerteventura, as it's much closer, but there they usually get picked up and taken to a centre. Then, if they aren't sent home, they try to get a flight to the mainland, so it's more of a gamble." He sighed. "I believe that some of the blokes who end up selling stuff on blankets do so because they're in debt to the same organisation that transported them here, but again, I never ask."

"Why not?"

"Partly because I don't want them to dwell on their debts, but mostly so I don't get tempted to give the ones I like a load of money. I contribute to our expenses fund, of course, but I'm not well enough off to go doling out hundreds of euros."

I thought about my swollen Contingency Fund, then remembered my £1000 wage, payable into my bank account at the end of each completed month at Peter's house. For the time being I'd have to go on paying £375 rent, my council tax, and other bills out of that, as well as trying to contribute to Peter's expenses, so I guessed I'd be left with three or four hundred pounds per month to play with.

On asking him about the expenses fund, he said it was mainly used to buy clothing, toiletries, cheap mobile phones, and bus fares for those who'd foolishly believed they'd be able to hitchhike to their destination. After wrestling with my conscience for a while, when we reached the foot of the lighthouse I told him I'd like to contribute to the fund.

"All in good time, Richie. Just a mo."

He trotted up the steps of the fine building at the base of the tower, weaved past a few waiting trippers, and went inside. He soon beckoned to me from the door.

"You're supposed to book a guided tour here, but Jorge always lets me nip up when I'm doing one of my exercise walks. Let's go."

After leaving his knapsack behind an information panel, Peter led the way up the spiral staircase. Although he took the steps two at a time, I kept up with him easily enough, me being a far younger man and used to tramping the Lancashire fells. After about a hundred steps I grinned on hearing him begin to breath more heavily, as my lungs were still functioning beautifully, and when he began to take one step at a time I considered nipping past the old fellow who was clearly trying to burn me off. A while later, however, my legs began to feel rather heavy, so I tried the two-step method in the hope of combating the lactic acid that was beginning to make a beeline for my quads and calf muscles. This extra effort got me panting just as much as the persistent Peter, who managed to put on a spurt towards the end and leave me trailing by a few feet.

On staggering out into the sunlight, I grasped the railings and cast a sidelong glance at the victor who soon began to do some stretching exercises.

"Those 344 steps really get to your legs in the end, don't they, Richie?"

"I'll say… they do."

"I come every few days and I usually do the climb two or three times."

I wiped my brow and shook the sweat from my hand. "I see."

"It makes up for the lack of hills. Besides, there's talk of holding a race up here, so I want to be ready for that." He slapped me on the back. "Don't worry, you'll soon leave me for dead if you come up often enough. It's a very specialised discipline, you see, not quite like climbing a normal hill."

"No." I wafted my legs with my baggy shorts and looked at the view for the first time, a remarkable panorama taking in the mouth of the Guadalquivir river to the north, the town, and the beaches stretching away to the south upon which my gaze lingered.

"Yes, it's along there where it all happens, Richie."

"Yeah."

"Do you think you'll be joining me when I go to do my next midnight walk?"

"Well…" I pictured us sitting on a sand dune in the dark, then trotting off to bundle an exhausted African into the back seat of Peter's Ford Focus. Not excessively difficult even for me. "Well, yes, I think I'd like to come along."

"Good lad. It's quite exciting and I think you'll enjoy it. I only hope they have a straightforward trip and none of them collapse on the beach. That makes things a bit trickier, as we have to decide if it's necessary to drive them to hospital or even call an ambulance, especially if they show any signs of hypothermia. From the hospital they'll usually be taken to the detention centre in Tarifa, cursing us for interfering."

I began to sweat again. "I see."

"It can compromise us too, because the police usually come with the ambulance. Many of us are still largely above suspicion, but fortunately we have a Danish doctor called Søren who doesn't give a shit if he gets caught."

"Why not?"

"Because he's brave. He's also sworn the Hippocratic Oath, of course, so if he happens to be on the beach when they arrive, he's obliged to help anyone who's ailing. Mari Carmen, a retired lawyer from El Puerto de Santa María, always stays with him, so with his oath and her legal jargon, on two occasions the cops ended up just telling them to clear off."

On noticing that I was eyeballing the distant beach in an anxious manner, Peter assured me that the boats' occupants, being generally young and fit, usually weathered the journey quite well and only suffered fatigue and dehydration due to the effects of seasickness.

"When migrant boats make the news it's usually because of some disaster, but the fact is that most of them arrive without any issues. Most of the boats have powerful outboard motors and make it here in as little as six hours, so on a calm night we see a lot of tired but smiling faces, as their European dream has finally begun."

"And you play a small but crucial part in making that dream come true," I murmured.

"That's right. Ha, the day after I've seen a lad off on his way, I strut around like a fighting cock who's just got laid."

I looked him up and down. "A disturbing image."

"Well, normally I'm just another pensioner bumbling around killing time, but after we've dropped Oumar off later I'll feel a great sense of satisfaction, and also relief, until the next one arrives. Come on, let's have a quick dip before we go back."

"Oh, I haven't brou–"

"Doesn't matter."

So after inspecting the huge halogen lamp above us, we walked down the 344 steps and onto the beach that was almost deserted due to the wind. After a bracing dip in my undies, I borrowed Peter's towel to rub myself down and I was soon striding homeward by his side, feeling sandy but pleased to have braved the waves on a day I would normally have deemed unsuitable for bathing.

Back at the house Oumar was strutting around like a fighting cock who had yet to get laid, so impatient was he to hit the road, so Peter said that after a bite to eat we'd drive both cars the seventy-odd miles to Seville airport, drop mine off, then take Oumar to the bus station. As I had yet to tell him about the doctor's note that I'd have to fly home to get, I muttered something about keeping the hire car for the time being, but Peter said it was such a stupid waste of money that I soon complied, as there'd be time enough to tell him that I intended to skive off five weeks' work.

That had been his daughter's idea, after all, and later on as I followed him along the dual-carriageway I pondered on the thorny question of whether or not to confess that I was being paid to keep an eye on him. I imagined that this admission wouldn't go down at all well, as Peter was a feisty chap who clearly didn't suffer fools or foolishness gladly, but as I knew I'd inevitably own up sooner or later, I decided to get it off my chest during the drive home, when we'd both be feeling chuffed to have successfully sent Oumar on his way to a better life.

With this better life in mind, on the way into Seville we both tried to convince the lad that he ought to pay his brother Idrissa in Madrid only a brief visit, before hopping on a bus to Zaragoza to join Moussa and his pals in their flat. There, we said, he'd have a far better chance of finding a proper job, rather than touting tat on a blanket for some mafia-like organisation, or simpler words to that effect.

"Yes, I want this," he said in Spanish. "But also I want Idrissa to come to Zaragoza."

I gasped. "A brilliant idea!"

"But not so simple," said Peter.

So in the car outside the large bus station we discussed the potential difficulties of such a move. As Idrissa had been reticent about his life in the capital, Oumar wasn't sure if he owed money to the people who supplied him with the goods he flogged, in which case he'd have to either pay up or do a bunk. Oumar thought this latter course – a daring idea that I'd suggested from the comfort of the passenger seat – too risky, as he believed the 'patrons', or bosses, would track him down and probably beat him up, before dragging him back to Madrid and thrusting a blanket into his hands.

"But if he owe no money, or not much, he can go with you to Zaragoza, no?" I said in my pidgin Spanish.

"Yes, if so, yes."

I turned to Peter. "Let's keep in touch and see what happens," I muttered in English. "If it's a question of a couple of hundred euros, I think I'd like to help him."

"Oumar has my number. We'll leave it at that for now."

"But…"

"Shush." He turned to face Oumar. "Are you ready to go?"

He exhaled noisily and cracked the knuckles of each hand. "Sí, vamos."

Peter told him to relax, as he was quite smartly dressed and wouldn't attract attention unless he looked nervous.

"OK."

"On the bus sit alone or, if that isn't possible, try to sit next to a young person, preferably a man. Understood?"

"Sí, Peter."

"If anyone speaks to you, smile a lot. You are visiting your brothers, so you are happy."

"OK."

"Will your brother meet you?" I asked.

He tapped the cheap phone which Peter had given him. "Yes, I think so."

"Text me whenever you want," said Peter.

"Sí. Muchas gracias, Peter… Richie." He sniffed. "C'est très, très gentil à vous."

Peter jumped out and opened the rear door, while I fetched Oumar's smallish travel bag from the boot. As we made our way into the terminal, Peter became very effusive, rambling on about all sorts of things and generally keeping Oumar's spirits up, because, as he later explained, the last thing he wanted was for any of us to become emotional in such a busy place. When Peter went to buy the ticket, I couldn't resist returning to the subject of trying to get Idrissa to accompany Oumar to Zaragoza. The lad had the presence of mind to point out the weakness of my reasoning, because he'd be sleeping on the sofa in Moussa's cramped flat, so the others might resent another new arrival. Also, Moussa had spoken to his boss about one brother, not two, so any slim chance Oumar had of getting a job in the furniture factory might be scuppered if the head of the family muscled in. At least that's what I think he was striving to convey, but I'd understood enough to realise that my well-intentioned interference was having a detrimental effect on his spirits, so I shut my gob just as Peter returned with the ticket to Madrid.

"Been blathering on, have you?" he muttered grimly.

"Sorry."

"I was the same the first time. OK, Oumar, vamos al autobus."

The bus wasn't too full and Oumar waved happily from his window seat, even blowing us a kiss before he disappeared from view.

"Job done."

"Yes, I hope he'll be all right."

"He's where he wants to be. Come on, let's get back to normality."

On the drive home Peter left me to ruminate for a while, before telling me that one of three things would now happen; he wouldn't hear another word from Oumar, he'd get a couple of texts before he became swept up in his new life, or they'd stay in touch, as had occurred with four of the seventeen men he'd hosted.

"Oumar's a good 'un and I sort of hope that'll happen, but for now we're going to try to put him out of our minds."

"Right," I said doubtfully.

"I mean it, Richie. If we spend our downtime fretting about one lad, we'll still have him on the brain when the next one arrives. We've done our bit for now, and that's that. Besides, there are support groups in the cities, mostly run by the Senegalese, so now it's time to think about yourself for a while."

"That's all I've done for the last forty-six years."

He chuckled. "It'll come easy to you then."

"Yes, I…" but I decided against spoiling the drive home by bringing up the subject of filthy lucre. "…I'm quite good at that."

5 – An Enlightening Walk

According to Elise, the 'walking' group leader who Peter had met only briefly on a handful of occasions, there were no boats scheduled to arrive in the coming days, so I was able to settle into my new home, potentially without a care in the world until a week on Tuesday – ten long days away – when I'd have to attend my local health centre and explain why I wasn't nor would be fit for work before my truncated library career officially ended. Denise had emailed me this news, as she'd been acting on my behalf during the early stages of my imaginary ailment, a chronic bad back which was so painful that I could barely walk, let alone lift anything as heavy as a library book. She'd even booked my return flight to Liverpool, but before I printed out my boarding passes I'd have to broach this delicate subject with my host.

On Saturday morning after a spot of gardening we set off along the beach to a campsite restaurant which Peter often frequented, as he found the five-mile walk just far enough to work up a healthy appetite, and the return journey ideal for burning off the calories he'd consumed. I'd never met such a fit seventy-two-year-old in my life before, as the oldsters in my rambling group had tended to stroll along at a sedate pace, but I was soon to learn that he was rather obsessive about his exercise regime. As well as hoofing it up the lighthouse about six times a week, he also walked about thirty miles, did press-ups, sit-ups and bicep curls every morning, and swam in the ocean whenever the waves or the outgoing tide didn't make it too dangerous.

That day a high of twenty-six degrees was forecast, but the westerly wind made it feel cooler.

"The wind can be a pain at times," Peter said as he loped along the beach barefoot. "But it has its benefits. Even in summer you can enjoy a morning or evening walk here, unlike on the Mediterranean coast where the heat and humidity are much worse."

A flurry of sand caused me to stop to rub my eyes.

"You'll soon learn to keep your sunglasses on." He prodded my still slimy arm. "What's with the lashings of suncream anyway? Don't you want to get a tan?"

"Yes, but not just yet."

"Oh."

As he'd detected my extreme protection, I had little choice but to spill at least a portion of the beans that were metaphorically weighing me down.

"Next week I have to fly home to get a doctor's note. Denise persuaded me… well, suggested that I skip my final weeks at work and come here. You'll understand that a lazy git like me didn't need much encouragement, even though I've enjoyed my years at the library," I said without pausing for breath.

"Well, well," he said as we resumed our walk.

"I'll catch a bus to Seville, a week on Monday," I mumbled.

"Oh, I think I'll be able to drive you there, unless we have a new guest who can't be left alone."

"Why would that be?"

"Well, I once left a chap in the house on his first day and he took it into his head to nick one of my cameras and bugger off."

"Oh, no," I said, shocked but also relieved by the change of subject.

"Fortunately most of my camera gear was locked up. He also stole a winter coat and a melon, which made it easy for my pals in the local police force to track him down. It was scorching hot, so a black man in a big coat with a melon under his arm was pretty easy to spot, the daft sod."

"So you called the cops?"

"Too right, but not the Civil Guard, of course."

"Well, well."

"What did you expect me to do? A thief's a thief, and the last thing the Senegalese want is someone like him giving them a bad name. The annoying thing was that here the justice system is so slow that they let him go, pending his trial, and he was never seen again."

"Why wasn't he sent to a detention centre?"

He shrugged. "Here the different official bodies don't communicate too well with each other. This has its good side for the migrants, so I just put that unfortunate episode down to experience. With the next two lads I left some money lying around to see if they'd take the bait, but I stopped doing that as it didn't seem right. Apart from that one thief, they've all treated me and my home with respect, but if we get another shifty one, I'll want to keep an eye on him."

"I've been meaning to ask you about your photography," I said, glad that the subject of my premeditated skiving had been put to bed for the time being.

"What about it?"

"Do you still do it?"

"I didn't for a long time."

During the next mile or so he told me that after the death of his wife he'd hurriedly brought his long career to a close and shoved all his gear in a cupboard, apart from an expensive new digital camera which he'd sold.

"In those early days of digital they made giant strides every year, so a two-grand camera body soon became obsolete. That's why I sold my Nikon, but I couldn't bear to part with all the film gear I'd had for so long. I even kept a broken old Leica, because I'd taken some honeymoon snaps on it, and the battered Contax that I started out with, but I had no desire to take photos until about four years ago, when I happened to mention my work to a bloke in the Betis bar and he asked me to do some family portraits for him.

"I was reluctant to dust off my gear, but he was a wealthy farmer and prepared to pay well for some real analogue prints, rather than the clinical digital stuff that most photographers were churning out. Anyway, I managed to buy some film and I took my Hasselblad and a couple of lights to his finca. I photographed his stuck-up wife and chubby kids well enough, and even found a proper lab in Madrid that made colour prints in the traditional way. I believe they usually just digitalise the negatives nowadays, so I was lucky… but I must be boring you to tears."

"Not at all," I said, pleased that he hadn't followed up my shameful revelation with any probing questions regarding my being in such a hurry to fly to his side that I'd had to cut my library career short. "Do go on."

"Well, I soon put my Hasselblad and other film equipment away and bought a decent Canon DSLR camera and a couple of lenses. That thief only pinched a cheap compact camera I'd left on the kitchen top, by the way. Since then, I've… well, this is something I'd prefer to show rather than tell you, so if you're interested, remind me when we get home."

"I will." I then trotted on ahead and turned to photograph him on my primitive phone camera. "Oh, it's blurred."

"Shutter speed too slow. I've still got a phone without a camera, so I don't waste my time taking pointless snaps. I'm still a bit out of love with photography, apart from this one thing I do. Come on, let's get a move on."

Despite these conversational distractions, I'd been examining the coastline as we walked and had so far found it to be more built up than it had looked from the top of the lighthouse. At times the coastal road appeared to head some way inland, behind a motley selection of buildings, so all in all the business of picking up arriving migrants seemed to be a good deal more complicated than I'd imagined. I mentioned this to Peter.

"What did you expect? That we'd sit on a bench and usher our lad into the car? No, it can be a bit trickier than that, as you'll find out, unless seeing the actual scene has changed your mind about coming along."

"Oh, no, I'm still up for it. In fact I hope a boat comes before I have to nip home."

"Why?"

"Er… well, to give me something to think about while I'm travelling, I suppose," I said weakly, because it had occurred to me that proving my worth before my departure might make Peter feel more lenient after I'd finally owned up to my dark monetary secret.

He just sniggered and broke into a jog.

Peter was greeted warmly at the rough and ready campsite restaurant and soon a steady stream of tapas, mostly of fish and seafood, began to arrive at our paper-covered plastic table in the shade.

"We can have meat for the main course, if you like," Peter said as I chewed doggedly on a rubbery piece of squid.

"Hmm."

"Though corvina al horno is their speciality, and it's delicious."

So we ate white sea bass cooked in the oven with potatoes, peppers, and enough garlic to repel the bloodthirstiest vampire. Peter washed his down with a large glass of cold white wine and I was pleased that he didn't try to persuade me to follow suit, because in that idyllic spot close to the sea, my arm wouldn't have needed much twisting.

"Now then," he said after we'd polished off our bowls of homemade ice-cream and ordered coffee.

"Now what?"

He smiled and flicked down his sunglasses to conceal his astute and somewhat unnerving blue eyes. "Why don't you unburden yourself of whatever it is you have to tell me?"

"Me?"

He looked around comically. "Can't see anyone else here, Rich."

"I prefer Richie."

"Richie."

"Although my mum and sister call me Richard."

"Oh, get *on* with it, then we can both relax."

Yes, I'll soon be relaxing on a last-minute flight back to Liverpool, I thought, but once I'd started to tell him about that fateful day in the library when Denise had proposed that I join her poor old dad, I found that by sticking to the facts I was able to relate the whole tale from beginning to end without telling a single fib.

"I can see you aren't too happy about what I've told you," I added after about a minute's silence.

"You can't even see my eyes."

"I can feel them, and your mouth's set like a… an angry person's mouth."

"I'm trying not to laugh."

"Really?"

"Or cry, or howl like a banshee." He slapped the table. "That bloody son of mine really has overstepped the mark this time."

"Hmm."

"Simon thinks that because he's made a lot of money he has a right to exercise power over everyone, not just his lackeys at work."

"Uh-huh."

"Just because I didn't bore myself to tears fussing over his spoilt kids for a whole week this summer, he's got it into that stubborn head of his that something's wrong with me, when I only used to stay longer because I had nothing better to do."

"Right."

He shook his head, before spitting gracefully onto the nearby sand. "And just imagine, actually *paying* you to come here to watch over me like a... a great lanky nanny."

I shrugged and sighed. "I know, it's never felt right. Luckily he hasn't coughed up yet, so I'll just tell him that you're absolutely fine and he needn't pay me anything."

"You must be joking."

"And if you want me to clear off, I'll under... what?"

"You heard." He rubbed his hands together and cackled in a most reassuring way. "Look, if the interfering sod's barmy enough to pay you, don't look a gift horse in the mouth, son."

"Yes, well, it doesn't seem quite ethical now that I've told you."

"Ethical my arse. Besides, I know how much he makes from that dealership and other businesses he's involved in, because he's conceited enough to tell me. No, a grand a month's nothing to him. He'd only waste it on more horses."

"Horses?"

"That's his latest hobby, though he's too scared to ride anything bigger than a pony. He wants his kids to go up in the world, you see, so he thinks that private schools and all the middle-class trappings will hide the fact that he's been a conniving wheeler-dealer ever since he left school. No, Richie, let the chump pay for your season in the sun."

"Oh, I don't know."

"Why not? You're about to do a bit of good for your fellow man, aren't you?"

"Well…"

"Which tickles me pink, to be honest, because Simon's a right racist so-and-so. Ha, just to think that his money will be indirectly helping a few deserving Africans to make something of themselves makes me feel all warm inside." He rubbed his flat brown belly to illustrate this. "Having said that, next week you might have to spin Denise some sort of yarn to justify staying here for any length of time."

My immense feeling of relief now became tempered by a couple of uncomfortable issues. As I hadn't told any fibs thus far, I didn't wish to sin by omission, so I admitted that Denise and his other two children would also be chipping in to pay my wages.

"Hmm, I see."

"And I find it hard to lie to Denise, because we're such good friends."

"Really good friends?"

"Yes."

"In that case you can come clean about our… complicity and simply stick whatever she pays you back into her bank account."

"That's true, but what about your other son and daughter?"

He knocked back his coffee and flapped a hand. "Bah, let's not split hairs about a few bob between friends. Simon'll have a job to get much out of Paul, as he's as tight as a duck's arse, and as for Adele, well, her and her twit of a husband make a packet flogging designer tableware and other expensive crap to numbskulls with more money than sense, so you could contribute that hundred quid or so, because it won't be more, to our expenses fund."

I laughed. "You don't mince your words when you're talking about your family, do you?"

He flipped up his sunglasses. "I don't mince my words, full stop. Oh, I'm as nice as pie to them when I'm there, and deep down I do love them, though not equally, but... well, life's too short to dither around, behaving like a perfect gent all the time." He reached over and grasped my hand, before pointing out to sea with his free one. "Here we've got a job to do, Richie, and we'll take any help we can get."

I gulped. "Yes."

"Now pay up and we'll be off."

As usually occurred after one of our key conversations, we remained mostly silent for some time as we trudged along the beach, each deep in thought. Peter didn't look dismayed after my confession, though I guessed he was ruminating on what to do about his meddlesome son. As for me, I felt a tad anxious about the fact that he now seemed to take my participation in the migrant scheme for granted, before I'd even set eyes on a single patera. I feared that if I were to wriggle out of my forthcoming commitments at some point, being paid a wage by Simon and the others would no longer seem acceptable to him. So it was that my least favourite four-letter word began to bug me for the first time since my arrival.

After we'd passed the last of the trees surrounding a golf course and reached the outskirts of town, I broke our silence by asking him what kind of work he thought I'd be able to do in Chipiona.

"I guessed you might be thinking along those lines."

"I bet you did. You've been thinking about Simon."

"Correct, and more precisely about what to do with him if he comes out to check up on me again. Last time I showed him the sights and generally kept him busy, but I can't be bothered to do that again. No, we'll just have to reassure him that thanks to your valuable assistance, I appear to be perfectly fine in body and mind."

"You are anyway."

"*I* know that, but we'll have to justify your presence, or he'll close the tap before long. Hmm, I think you're going to have to take Denise into your confidence and tell her exactly what the score is, migrants and all. Either that or say that I'm ever so slightly barmy and will need watching from now on. What do you reckon's the best way?"

"I'm a poor liar, and she'll probably prise the truth out of me anyway." I looked at the town where so many industrious people were earning their daily bread. "It'd be better if I could get some sort of work. Then I could support myself and tell Denise that I no longer need a wage." I mused on the leisurely winter which stretched out before me. "Maybe in the spring, but no later than that."

He sniggered. "That's the spirit. Anyway, you won't need to worry about being talent-spotted too soon, because you haven't a hope in hell of finding a job before next Easter."

I tried to turn my relieved sigh into a gentle groan.

"Unless you want to slave in a greenhouse and earn about forty euros a day. I think I could arrange that for you."

"Well, I..."

"But I can tell you now that you wouldn't last two hours. They work fast in those places, harvesting the veg, and even in winter it can be as hot as hell."

"How do you know?"

"That farmer I took some photos for gave me a guided tour. It was May and you should have seen the sweat pouring off those Moroccan blokes. There were two black Africans among them – from Mali, I believe – and they seemed to stand the heat a bit better, but a soft Brit like you wouldn't last half an hour."

"My endurance is diminishing as we speak. I once worked in a foundry, you know. The last proper one in Accrington."

"How long were you there?"

"About nine months. They let me go because I didn't know Sage and couldn't be bothered to learn it."

"What's that?"

"Accounting software. I was in the office, you see, but it still got quite warm in summer."

He laughed. "Nice one."

"I guess I'll have to skip the greenhouses. Is there really nothing else I could do?"

"Not till Easter when the trippers start to come in greater numbers, and even then it won't be easy. There are plenty of youngsters here to work in the bars and restaurants, but I might be able to get you a trial somewhere."

I recalled my short stint at a cafe in Colne, back in the days before machine-made coffee began to attract a more eclectic clientele. I'd served pie and peas with mugs of tea to workers who mocked the grubby apron I was obliged to wear. After three months I was back at the Job Centre, begging John – then a younger and less embittered man – to find me a cushy number at the town hall.

"I'll really need to find something to do all year round, if I'm to make a life for myself in Spain."

"Hmm, all year round… ah!" He tapped his bronzed forehead. "Bloody hell, I'd forgotten the most obvious thing of all."

"What's that?"

"Teaching English, of course. I believe there's a great demand for it these days, and in Chipiona I only know of a couple of crummy language schools that have their shutters down half the time."

"So should I try to get a job at one of them?"

"No, you'd be better off going it alone. You'd charge by the hour and go and teach the kiddies in their own homes."

I cringed. "Kiddies?"

"The parents want their kids to learn English, so they'll have more options when they're older. It's all the rage nowadays, and a tall handsome Englishman like you would be a real hit. There was a Swedish bloke doing it for a while, but his accent was worse than that Sven-Goran Eriksson's and I don't think he had much success. I'm sure you'd get on well with the kiddies, and the mummies too, I wouldn't wonder."

"Yes, well, there's just one problem. I'm not a teacher."

"Pah, who cares about that? I believe you have the makings of one anyway."

"And I don't speak Spanish properly yet."

"You know a damn sight more than they'll know English, and before long you'll be speaking reasonably well, especially if you study as hard as you say you're going to."

"Oh, I will, once I get time to open a book." I pictured myself in a pleasant parlour with a couple of well-behaved kids, sipping coffee that their charming mummy had made me. "Yes, it's definitely an option that I ought to think about."

"Just say the word and I'll start to make a few enquiries."

"Not till I get back from England. Then I'll have a better idea of where I stand, and… and…"

"And how long you'll be able to live the life of Riley, eh?"

"Hmm."

He loped ahead then turned to face me. "Look, as far as I'm concerned, you've just started a sabbatical that I guess you deserve. You worked at the library for nearly six years, which must be a record for you."

"It is, by a long way."

"Right, so try to chill out and enjoy yourself for now."

"All right."

"All I want you to do is give me a hand with the migrants until the boats stop coming. Then will be the time to look at the bigger picture, but for now carpe diem and to hell with earning a living, OK?"

I was becoming fonder of Peter all the time.

6 – Goodbye to All That

On our arrival home Peter told me that he'd prefer to explain his photography project to me some other time, and we spent the rest of the day each doing our own thing. I had a little desk in my spacious room which overlooked the patio, so I arranged my Spanish books ready for the intensive studying that was to commence the very next day, before lying down to read, snooze, then read some more till Peter summoned me down for a bite of supper.

During the following sunny and not overly windy days we got into a pleasant routine which suited me just fine, because fortunately I was just about fit enough to keep up with my indefatigable host, although I missed his early morning exercise routine due to my failure to rise in time. After a fruit and cereal-based breakfast, we always headed for the beach and walked briskly for an hour, before repairing to one cafe or another for coffee and a restorative snack. It soon dawned on me that he had no particular favourite place, choosing to spread his custom around the hostelries close to the seafront. It may have been my imagination, but wherever we went there seemed to be two or three people who glowered at Peter and had a good old mutter, so I suspected that his clandestine activities were more or less common knowledge and frowned upon by the more conservative elements. One day two moustachioed oldies looked like they were about to approach our table, but when Peter flipped up his shades and eyeballed them gravely they had a change of heart and made for the door. When I broached the subject in a roundabout way, he said my mind must be playing tricks on me and that we visited different places so that I could see them all, so I didn't pursue the matter any further.

Back home I normally went to my room to study for a while, then after a healthy lunch and a short siesta we hit the beach once again, every other day by way of the lighthouse which he made me climb two or three times, though not quite as fast as on that first excruciating occasion. During our second walk of the day Peter invariably whipped off his top and plunged into the sea in his running shorts, so I had little choice but to brave the choppy waves and chilly water. As I thrashed around I wondered if these evening plunges would go on beyond October, but I didn't ask, because since our conversation during the long beach walk Peter had become a man of fewer words, so I opted to play the strong, silent type and refrain from whining about trivial things or speculating on my future.

After hurrying home and showering, Peter cooked something simple but appetising for supper, then watched Spanish TV for about an hour before hitting the sack. I stayed up for a while longer, sometimes putting the English subtitles on an American film dubbed into Spanish in order to practise my listening comprehension, though I rarely watched one to the end due to the interminable adverts which I also strove to decipher. On climbing the stairs at around midnight, I developed a strange habit of always trying the door of the fourth bedroom which, as far as I knew, had remained locked since my arrival. Therein lay Peter's photographic gear, I assumed, and it might well be the place where his project took place, but as he was yet to enlighten me, I'd just have to wait and see what he got up to beyond that door.

So the days passed by and the much anticipated message from Elise about the next boat failed to arrive, prompting me to suspect that Peter may have exaggerated their regularity, though if he'd hosted seventeen Senegalese men since the spring, surely another patera would be due soon.

"It'll be sod's law if a boat comes during my four days away," I said as we sipped coffee in yet another new venue, a restaurant down by the port, which is divided into two sections, one for fishing boats and another for leisure craft.

He smiled. "Sod's law or a stroke of luck?"

I told him that I sincerely wanted a boat to arrive before my departure because it would help me to decide whether or not to follow Denise's advice and give up my flat.

"What the hell has one thing got to do with another?"

"Well, it's a big decision to make. It's a good flat and I doubt I'll ever find another for the price I'm paying. It's a bit soon to commit myself to a life in Spain, but to keep it is going to cost me over five hundred quid a month. As Denise says, it's a daft amount to be paying if I'm not going to be there."

He tutted impatiently. "I'll rephrase my question. What have the boats got to do with you giving up your flat?"

"Well, if I can't hack this migrant business, I might regret it."

"Why?"

I shrugged like a guilty schoolboy. "If I end up chickening out of the pickups, you might not want a big wuss like me around for too long. Then there's the wage that you don't mind me getting... as long as I pull my weight."

"Bloody hell, Richie, you're like a scratched record. You can't justify the wage anyway, but you're prepared to take it. Look, the migrants will be staying at my house in any case, and whether you come with me to pick them up or not is no big deal."

I nodded and emitted a non-committal sort of sound from the back of my throat.

He smiled. "After all, that sort of thing isn't for everyone."

"No."

"Some people take a little adventure like that in their stride. They even relish it, whereas others hate to step out of their comfort zone." He pointed at half a dozen fishing boats lined up along the quayside. "For the blokes who go out in those in all weathers, driving an African to town at three in the morning would feel like a night off." He pointed at the posh leisure boats in front of us. "While for some of these affluent types who've made their money sat on their arses, they'd laugh at the idea of going out of their way to help anyone less fortunate than themselves."

"I'm neither a brave fisherman nor a selfish capitalist."

"No, but the trouble with you is that you don't know what you are. You've drifted along for so many years that you're in danger of... coasting towards retirement and death without ever having pushed yourself."

I snorted. "I push myself up those lighthouse steps every time you drag me up them."

"I don't drag you. I breathe down your neck so you don't slow down."

"I... I walked seventeen miles one day this summer. No-one made me do that."

"Bully for you. Did you feel good afterwards?"

"Yes, tired but pleased that I'd done it."

"There you are then. Effort equals satisfaction."

"Hmm."

He patted his sinewy thighs. "You probably think I'm nuts to do so much exercise at my age, but I get up every morning and that's what I feel like doing. It gives me a buzz, but in my experience, altruistic effort equals even greater satisfaction." He grinned. "I could have my migrants delivered to my door, you know."

"Really?"

"Yes, some of the group members do that, as they're too old or infirm to be racing up and down beaches. In a couple of cases they just don't fancy it, but that's all right, because there are about a dozen of us who do the risky work to get them off the beach, as you'll see, unless you chicken out when the time comes, but that's all right too, because God didn't create all men alike, after all."

"All right, all right," I snapped. "Now I *really* want a boat to come before I go, just to show you I'm no chicken."

"That's the spirit. Your turn to pay."

After pulling out my wallet I impulsively ransacked it and handed him four €20 notes. "That's my first contribution to the fund, and there'll be plenty more."

"Ta." He slipped the notes into his shorts pocket. "Let's hope that my Simon sells plenty of cars."

When he began to cackle, I followed suit, as it seemed like the right thing to do.

Alas, no boat was scheduled to arrive before my departure, and nor was the fourth bedroom opened, so I flew home in an undecided frame of mind; undecided about whether to throw in my lot with Peter or consider the option of striking out alone before I'd outworn my welcome.

Despite my best efforts with the suncream, I'd acquired a rather nice tan and had also rid myself of a stubborn ring of fat around my waist, so on meeting me at Liverpool airport Denise jokingly opined that a couple of weeks in Spain had transformed me from a pale library lizard into a bronzed beachboy.

I can see that here a writer of my ilk – a somewhat indolent one, let's face it – is in danger of droning on about his short UK stay for a whole chapter when the curious reader may be itching to get back to Chipiona to see what's in store for him. For this reason I'll omit the fascinating conversations I had with Denise, her brother Simon, my sister Cathy, my dear old Mum, and the sceptical lady doctor, and merely state the facts in as succinct a manner as I'm able.

As soon as I entered the flat that had sheltered me from the slings and arrows of my outrageously idle life, I knew the time had come to pack up my things and move on. It had served me well for nigh on fifteen years, and in it I'd lazed, loved, studied, and given little thought to the fact that it was a titchy, dismal sort of place without a view of anything worth seeing. Peter's spacious orangey-pink house, on the other hand, though it didn't boast a sea view, was an airy, well-lighted place – especially with the blinds up – where there was room to roam without getting under each other's feet.

Peter, although a veritable human dynamo, wasn't getting any younger, and if we got on well in the longer term, what was to stop me from being his faithful companion during his late autumn and winter years? That could be a good way of spending the potentially problematic period until I received my state pension in relative comfort, I thought as I waited for my trusty old kettle to boil, before recalling Peter's recent words about the danger of me coasting towards retirement and death without ever having pushed myself.

My God, he was right! And how awful of me to think of my new pal as merely a means to such a pathetically unambitious end. Even before brewing the tea that I was simply gagging for, I grabbed a pen and a dusty post-it pad and wrote the following:

THINGS YOU MUST DO:
Help Peter with the migrants ~~to the best of your abil~~ *as much as you can.*
Study Spanish for at least three hours every day, not including telly.
Get out and meet people.
Look into this English teaching thing.
Look into other work opportunities.
Show interest in Peter's photography project when you find out what it is.
Don't discount the possibility of relocating to a place where there is (interesting) work to be had, preferably not too far from Chipiona.
Be prepared to act if/when Peter shows signs of getting pissed off with your presence.
In this case, accelerate most of the above.

Then, after a well-earned cuppa, I neatly copied my scribbling onto a sheet of paper, folded it, and placed it in my wallet, happy with my firm but not overly specific resolutions.

Energised by my dynamism, I then set about deciding what to do with all the stuff that I'd accumulated over the years. With yet more post-its I labelled items of furniture that I'd invite one of the local charity shops to collect, before remembering that my mother's third bedroom was half-empty and no longer used, so there was nothing to stop me shoving everything in there, just in case I ended up returning from Spain with my figurative tail between my legs.

"No, no, no," I said to my big living room mirror, before slapping a post-it on it and everything else, except a neat little table which was said to be Victorian and worth a bob or two.

I was similarly ruthless with all my appliances, kitchenware, and most of my clothes, shoes, and other bits and bobs. I even culled my large collection of books, setting aside the work of authors who I no longer liked, so I ended up with about four hundred tomes – well, mostly paperbacks – which I'd take to my mum's and thence to Spain, once I'd established myself at Peter's or in a place of my own.

The next morning I didn't renege on my bold decision and called two charity shops who would have to fight over my worldly good. In the event their representatives arrived at roughly the same time and each tried to convince the other to take the belongings that in the clear light of day didn't look up to much, but by using all my powers of persuasion, and giving both of the grizzled volunteers twenty quid to spend as they wished, I managed to empty the flat of everything that I couldn't take back with me to Spain, bar the books and the table which I took to my mother's – in my sister's car – where I installed myself for the remainder of my stay.

I shall now go back on my promise not to yatter on about this English interlude and reproduce a mere snippet of conversation between my mum and me.

"So now you're homeless, Richard."

I sniggered. "Oh, I wouldn't say that, Mum."

"I would. When you come back you'll not be able to stay here for long. You know we get on each other's nerves after a while, so you'll just have to get another flat and start over again... from scratch," she said, the final bit being a barbed reference to my wanton disposal of a lot of perfectly serviceable furniture and a fine washing machine that she herself had given me.

"From now on I'll only be coming home on holiday, Mum."

She tutted and shook her head. "Nay, a leopard can't change its spots, and neither can a lazy lad like you. If you struggle to hold down a job here, how are you going to do it abroad?"

I ignored this uncompromising question and told her that her daughter Cathy was more optimistic about my chances of survival in the big wide world.

"Humph!"

"Yes, I've told her my story so far and she says that I seem to have landed on my feet. I also showed her my new reso... a few notes that I wrote about what I'm going to do, and she says that if I can stick to that, with any luck I won't need to return to the shitty life I was leading before the library."

"Language!"

"Your daughter's words, not mine."

"You'll not be able to stay in that old fella's house forever, you know."

"I *know* that, Mum."

"Then there'll be all the paperwork and lots of other fuss and bother that folk who go to Spain have to go through, not to mention this Brexit business, if it ever happens, and you'll have no place to run to when you lose your next job... except here."

"I'm aware of all that." I flexed a golden bicep. "And I'll take it in my stride."

She wrinkled her nose and flicked back a wisp of grey hair. "Unless, of course, that old fella does let you stay on."

"Well, he might, you know."

She stood up and folded her arms around her ample waist. "He'd better, or, as your dad would have said, you'll be buggered."

"Language."

She smiled. "His words, not mine. Now get yourself off to that doctor's, else they'll pay you nowt when you finish."

"Blimey, is that the time?"

After legging it to the health centre I used the space between the inner and outer doors to transform myself from a svelte sprinter into a doubled-up piece of human wreckage, but I needn't have worried, because Denise knew the doc and it was no skin off her rather cute nose to sign me off for another three weeks, thus officially terminating the best job I'd ever had.

The attractive thirtysomething doctor with lovely long brown hair got me thinking about womankind in general, so after taking a seat in the cafe I'd patronised for more years than I cared to remember, I pondered on the likelihood of my finding a suitable girlfriend in the not-too-distant future. My story so far may have given you the impression that I'm something of a ladies' man, and I won't deny that my passably handsome face, relative slimness, and pleasant, easy manner had enabled me to 'score' more often than most, but age waits for no man. The fact that I'd had to settle for the not especially attractive pest-control operative brought it home to me that as I approached fifty with my rapidly receding hairline and far from perfect teeth, I was unlikely to pull any more stunners who would put up with my lack of achievements and ambition.

No, I didn't aspire to attract a lady as gorgeous and accomplished as that doctor, but I hoped that a nice divorcee whose kids had grown beyond the tiresome stage (0-16) might still find a man like me appealing enough to invite me into her life and maybe even the home she owned. I'd never been a sponger, by the way, unless you call spending every weekend in the warmth of Julie the teacher's house sponging, but I'd usually picked up the tab during our outings and had nobly refused to move in, as I'd known deep down that ours wasn't a love to last a lifetime.

I considered adding 'especially women' to my resolution to get out and meet people, but as I'd found during the last thirty years that opportunity generally comes knocking when you least expect it, I chose not to do so. As for Peter's hint that the mummies of my hypothetical students might be up for a spot of extracurricular frolicking, well, I'd never gone in for married women and had no intention of sullying my fairly honourable amorous record at a time in my life when I hoped to become a better and more go-ahead sort of guy.

This got me thinking about Peter's attitude to the fair sex. From the lateral movements of his sunglasses I'd deduced that he still admired the female form, especially if it were topped by a pretty face, but he'd made no mention of any relationships and was still apt to sigh whenever he spoke of his late wife. I decided to ask him if he was on the lookout for a suitable lady or if he intended to go on with his somewhat ascetic life. Were he to find a new partner, my ongoing companionship would become superfluous to his needs, but I resolved to put my pal's interests first and encourage him to flip up his shades more often whenever he came across a physically appealing middle-aged señora who wasn't wearing a wedding ring. In this way I might also recharge my own love radar, which had been practically powered off since my tryst with the rat catcher.

Anyway, here I am, waffling away rather than moving on to describe the most eventful week in my life since I got stuck in a crevice on a camping trip to the Yorkshire Dales at the tender age of twelve. Had there been internet in the early eighties, you'd still be able to find virtual press cuttings about my incredible stoicism while I spent three whole hours clinging to the limestone cliff until the mountain rescue team arrived to hoist me up and into the limelight for a few thoroughly enjoyable days. Since then nothing had come close to equalling this event for sheer exhilaration and a feeling of being at the centre of things, but that was about to change.

Before I whisk you back to Chipiona I ought to slot in a few words about my two meetings with Denise, one at the library and the other at the least bad restaurant in town where I invited her to dinner. In her workplace, as well as chatting about library-related matters, I spoke in general terms about the great time I'd been having with her totally compos mentis dad, without mentioning Oumar or anything else to do with the migrant business. I then arrived at the Italian eatery fully intending to make a clean breast of things, but Peter had beaten me to it, as in the meantime he'd called her and, on realising that I'd been too cowardly to spill the beans, brought her up to speed regarding his activities and my intention to help out from now on.

Denise and I spoke for a long time about this, but I'll only quote what was said between cheesecake and coffee.

"Simon mustn't hear a single word about the migrants, Richie."

"No, he won't. When he called me yesterday I rambled on about our beach walks and so on until he butted in and asked me point blank if I thought his dad was losing his marbles. I said he seemed fine, but that he might be overdoing the exercise, especially the lighthouse climbs. This seemed to worry him, as if he couldn't imagine a man of his age being able to do something like that."

"Simon weighs about seventeen stone and does no exercise at all. He already takes statins and his private doctor's been warning him about diabetes."

"Right. Anyway, my... fortuitous words seemed to do the trick and now he's sort of transferred his worries from your dad's mental health to his physical wellbeing."

She smiled. "That's all right then. Simon just likes to feel in control, so whenever he calls you could tell him that you're monitoring his exercise regime and keeping him in check, or something like that. If you keep Dad in the loop too, that ought to satisfy Simon for quite a while."

"OK." I then asked her to give me her bank details, so I could pay back the £100 per month she was expected to contribute to the Keep Richie in Chipiona Fund.

"Put it in the walking group's expenses fund for now."

"All right, thanks, but what about Paul and Adele's contributions?"

"Paul refuses to pay, and Adele wouldn't mind if she knew what you were up to, which she won't, as we can't risk Simon finding out."

"OK, I'll put your and Adele's two hundred in the fund and another two hundred of my own... of Simon's money too. I'll probably pay your dad something for my room and board as well."

She giggled. "Save some money too, Richie, as you don't know what tomorrow will bring."

I pictured the Atlantic as it darkened of an evening and agreed that I certainly didn't.

7 – M-Day

"Keep your head down!" Peter hissed as a searchlight panned over the shallow sand dune in which we were hiding.

"Sorry. Er, seeing as the civil guards seem to be on to us, shouldn't we sort of... scuttle off?"

"What, and just leave the migrants to get picked up?"

"We might get picked up too," I said, before picturing all the furniture I'd have to buy back from the charity shops after I'd been deported.

He growled. "They can't possibly know for sure that a boat's due to arrive."

"Someone might have informed them."

"Not one of us."

"They could have intercepted the texts."

"Don't be daft. It's the Spanish Civil Guard we're talking about, not the KGB. It's my guess that it's just a routine patrol, so hopefully they'll clear off soon."

"I'm glad you parked up that track and not on the road like I suggested."

"All our cars will be out of sight," he said, as the twelve seasoned members plus the raw recruit were covering about two kilometres of the coastline, as requested by one of the smuggling crew members who was in touch with Elise. Peter had chosen a spot near the campsite restaurant we'd visited, so that I'd have a better idea of the lie of the land. On that wonderfully moonlit night we could see far out to sea, where during the last hour only a couple buoys had been bobbing in the choppy water, but when another faint form appeared beyond them, Peter said he hoped the guards would stop messing around with their searchlights and sod off back to their barracks.

"And what if they don't?"

"They usually do."

"Oh, so is this normal?"

"This is the fourth time it's happened since I joined the pickup team."

"You didn't mention that."

"Didn't want to worry you." He peered out to sea. "Yes, it looks like a patera. Oh, listen."

We heard two or three vehicles accelerating away towards Chipiona.

"Thank God for that." He chuckled. "It gets the old heart racing, doesn't it?"

I pressed an artery in my neck. "Yes. I'll be glad when it's over."

"Oh, it should be plain sailing now. They'll have had a fairly calm crossing, so it'll just be a question of grabbing our man, pointing the others towards our colleagues, then getting back to the car and driving home."

"With an African who's just arrived in his promised land," I thought aloud.

"They're normally shattered. We'll put ours to bed, drive him to Seville in a day or two, then get back to our lazy life."

I remembered the lighthouse steps which we'd climbed eight times since my return from England six days earlier. Peter had been tickled by the fact that his obese son was now more concerned about his excessive exercising than his mental faculties, and we'd agreed that I'd claim to be struggling to slow him down, while he'd complain that I was a terrible fusspot. In this way we hoped to keep my wages coming in until Easter, when I fully intended to find myself a job and tell Simon that his dad was finally cured of his exercise addiction. Six months spent siphoning off a small part of his income was enough, we'd agreed, and by then Denise and Adele would have made a handsome contribution to the fund and ought to be spared any more expense, although I intended to offer Denise a dual refund every month, as it still didn't seem right to take a hundred quid from each of them towards a charitable endeavour not of their own choosing.

Peter stood up and slapped the sand from his legs. "It looks like the boat's going to reach the beach a bit further south. Let's get going."

"It's still a long way out."

"They'll put a spurt on now. They'll be keen to get shut of their cargo and head for home."

"Another six hours."

"At least."

Sticking to the uppermost part of the beach, we passed two tracks leading to a few chalets, before Peter led me onto a patch of wasteland where we sat close to some stunted bushes.

"We're away from the main road now, so if the cops come back they'll probably miss this bit with their damned searchlights. I'm not sure how much they know about what we get up to, but they're probably grateful."

"Why's that?"

"Well, we whisk the migrants away and get them out of the province. If it weren't for us, there'd be reports of Africans wandering all over the place and they'd have their work cut out to round them up. Like other Spanish funcionarios, or civil servants, they have a job for life and mean to make it as easy as possible. You'll find out how bloody lazy they are when you start to sort out your paperwork, as from what you've told me about your flat, it sounds like you're planning on staying in Spain."

"Yes, I've burnt my bridges to some extent. I hope I don't get caught and have to quickly rebuild them."

"From your precious contingency fund, eh?" he said with a laugh, and if us talking casually about these mundane matters at such a nerve-wracking time sounds a bit strange, it dawned on me later that Peter was deliberately keeping my mind off the task at hand, just as he'd nattered on to Oumar at the bus station to prevent him from displaying his anxiety.

When a light flashed briefly from the boat whose outboard motor was now audible, I made to stand up, but Peter pulled me down and told me we'd be staying put until the migrants stepped into the water.

"That lad Cheikh I told you about arrived on a moonlit night too. He said it was amazing to see all these figures appear out of nowhere and take them off one by one. They'd expected to have to lie low somewhere till morning, then try to get to a town without being spotted. That was about four months ago, but now they know we'll probably be here for them, thanks to Elise."

"And the smugglers, presumably."

"Just one of them, I believe. He must feel a sense of solidarity with the migrants, though I don't know anything about him. The group never meets up, you see, but when it's all over Elise says we're going to have a big dinner to celebrate all the good work we've done."

"When the authorities clamp down on this bit of coastline, you mean?"

"Yes, at some point they'll start using patrol boats and helicopters, so once the smugglers lose a patera or two, they'll choose somewhere else. The keener members might be prepared to drive further to go on helping, but I've decided that once they're done here, I'm done too. I am seventy-two, after all. Right, let's go."

To my amazement, Peter's chatter had made me unaware that the boat had reached shallow water about two hundred yards away and dark figures could be seen climbing over the side. As we hurried along I saw other people converging on the boat in ones and twos, then Peter gasped and uttered a profanity too rude for me to reproduce in these pages of family reading.

"What's up?"

"Christ, have you seen the number of people getting out?

"Oh, yes, there do seem to be quite a lot of them."

"The bastards! This is the sort of thing you see on telly, but it hasn't happened here before. There must be thirty… even forty of the poor buggers in that little thing."

I wailed faintly. "So what do we do?"

"Looks like you'll be sleeping on the settee, and me on the floor, unless… hey, Elise!"

A stout lady in her sixties wearing commando-style gear approached and shone a weak torch on our faces, then on her own calm countenance.

"Hi, Peter. Hello, Richie, thank you for coming."

I nodded and gurgled some sort of reply.

"Tonight they have been too greedy." She scanned the scene of splashing people and nodded slowly. "You must take two."

"We could take three," said Peter.

"Two is enough. Get him and him. Good luck."

Peter stepped into the surf and grabbed the arm of flailing young man, so I followed and groaned on feeling my newish trainers fill with seawater, as I'd rather hoped to greet our single guest on the nice dry sand.

"Bonjour," I said to the slim young chap I accosted, though it was still only about three o'clock. On seeing the glint of his big white teeth, I also smiled, before taking his heavy rucksack and grasping his arm until we reached the shore. The four of us were soon walking briskly along the beach. As my lad was shivering, I rubbed his back through his thin damp coat and muttered a few multilingual words of encouragement. Our other guest seemed to be in fine fettle and insisted on taking his travel bag from the old geezer by his side. As we neared the campsite I began to experience a mild feeling of euphoria.

Now all that remained was to nip along a track past a few deserted chalets, across the main road, then along another track to the car. Within half an hour we'd be bundling them into the house and I'd trot upstairs to run a hot bath; not for me, of course, as I'd simply wash my feet in the bidet, but for my lad who was still shivering despite the mildness of the night. Just then I felt glad that we'd taken two of them, as it meant I hadn't just come along for the ride. I was already looking forward to making their short stay a pleasant and reassuring one, before we drove them to Seville and waved them off on the bus. The fact that Oumar had so far sent Peter only two short texts didn't bother me in the least, because Peter and I were simply selfless intermediaries who required little thanks for our sterling services. Ah, yes, it felt really fine to be helping my fellow man, and those searchlights and the packed patera had certainly added a bit of extra spice to an already extraordinary event for a lazybones like me. I almost regretted that I didn't have children and would consequently have no grandchildren to dandle on my knees and entertain with my tales of derring-do, so I'd have to make do with my niece and nephew...

"Get down!" Peter yelled. "À terre!" he added, though his dive made it clear what was expected of us.

A searchlight had been switched on, aiming directly along the track we were just about to reach, so the civil guards hadn't gone home after all, but had sneakily lain in wait for the prey they must surely have been expecting.

"Someone's tipped them off," I said, before spitting out some sand.

"You may be right, Sherlock. Let's just hope they can't be arsed to get out of the jeep." He twisted his head around. "Damn it, they've come down another track along there too. Looks like they mean business this time."

"What can we do?" I whimpered.

"Don't move a muscle. Restez-vous complètement immobile."

"Oui, Monsieur," said my young companion whose back I continued to rub.

"Keep still, you pillock!" Peter muttered.

"He's cold."

"The sand's warm. Be patient. Il faut être patient, mes amis."

"They haven't moved the searchlight."

"They'll be having a fag in the jeep. If they seriously wanted to catch us, they'd have left the lights off and come creeping down the beach, but they obviously can't be arsed, the lazy bastards."

"You don't seem too fond of them."

"Oh, all they do in Chipiona is slap fines on folk for driving while using their mobiles, whether they are or not. One mate of mine was scratching his beard and they pulled him over. He showed them his phone was switched off in the glove compartment, but they still fined him. The local police are all right, as most of them are from Chipiona, but the civil guards get posted here from all over the place and they couldn't care less what people think of them. They're nowhere near as notorious as they were during Franco's time, but anyone who joins is a bit suspect in my eyes."

Peter's diversionary murmuring tactic seemed to sooth the two lads, who were now breathing more softly, but choosing this moment to mention the military police force famed for its brutality throughout most of its 170-year history did little to calm my own nerves.

"We'll soon be in their cellar with thumbscrews on," was my feeble attempt at a joke.

He chuckled. "I might be, but you three are going to crawl down to the sea, then set off walking along the beach."

"All the way home?"

"If necessary, but I hope to pick you up at some point. When you see headlights flash three times, it'll be me, not them." He sighed. "Now I'll have to try to find a way past them."

"Could you go through the campsite?"

"Hmm, I can try, but I think the main gates might be a bit high for an old duffer like me to get over."

"I suppose you could lie low near the restaurant for a while."

"I'll play it by ear."

My lad had stopped shivering, but he was lying a bit too still for my liking. When I squeezed his arm he groaned and seemed to cling to the sand as if it were a soft mattress.

"Peter, there's no way he can walk five miles in his condition."

"Comment vas-tu?" he asked the other lad.

"Je me sens bien. Estoy bien."

"Ah, hablas español."

"Un poco."

Peter then explained that he and his strong English friend – meaning me – would have to help the other man walk up to eight kilometres along the beach, though he hoped to pick us up on the way.

"Está bien. Vamos."

Peter shoved his knapsack into my ribs. "There's water and a big flask of coffee and some pastries in there, and a windproof jacket."

I chuckled mirthlessly. "You didn't mention you'd brought all that."

"Didn't want to worry you, but I knew something like this might happen one day. Right, get well away from here before you stop for a rest. With any luck I'll meet you just past the golf course, where the road reaches the beach again."

"I didn't bargain for this."

"Are you man enough to do it, or do we have to lie here all night while they snooze in their jeep?"

I snorted. "Of course I'm up for it." I turned onto my side and managed to get a knapsack strap over my shoulder. "Vámonos," I said with the authority of a seasoned arctic explorer, before leading the way towards the sea on my hands and knees.

Beyond the reach of the searchlight we stood up and began to squelch slowly along the shoreline. For a while the younger lad walked erectly between us. He'd donned the windproof jacket and I began to feel hopeful that within half an hour we'd be piling into Peter's car, but his wet legs soon became wobbly and we had to support him from either side to keep him moving along.

"El mucho vomitar en barco," my athletic comrade told me.

"One kilometre more and we stop for coffee and food," I said in Spanish, feeling increasingly like an army officer in the heat of battle. I was well-rested and fully fed and watered, of course, and I saw it as my duty to keep their spirits up by adopting an authoritative and confident tone, as if this were a mere nocturnal walk in the park for me. If truth be told, after the fright of the searchlight I was beginning to enjoy myself again. I felt sure that Peter would manage to slip past the dozy, despicable civil guards, so the ordeal the youngster was suffering oughtn't to last much longer. Then I would bathe him and tuck him into bed, and in years to come he would often refer to the fatherly figure who had saved his bacon on that moonlit night in the south. By then he'd be a father himself, prospering in some Spanish city or with his own business back in Dakar, and he'd dandle his children on his knees and tell them that their good life had been made possible by that stoical Englishman who'd fearlessly led him to safety...

Then he collapsed in a heap on the sand, so I put my fantasy on hold and soon managed to get a little sweet coffee down his throat, though he spat out a piece of pastry and lay groaning on his side.

"I carry him," said my valiant lieutenant.

"No, I will carry him."

By way of reply he tensed a large bicep close to my eyes and in no time we had the lad clinging to his broad back and he began to march doggedly along the firm sand. Up ahead I pointed out the lights of a roundabout and said that Peter might be waiting for us there but, alas, on scanning the coast road there were no car headlights to greet us. With about three miles still to go I suspected we were in for the long haul, so I decreed a rest break and encouraged the sturdy porter to drink some coffee and eat his fill of pastries, while I made do with a few sips of water. The ailing boy also drank some coffee and managed to hold down a little food. He then walked about half a mile between us before sinking to his knees once again.

"Now I will carry him," I said as I handed over the knapsack.

"OK, you carry a little."

The lad can't have weighed much more than eight stone and for a while I bore my burden more easily than I'd expected to, as all those lighthouse steps I'd climbed must have strengthened my thighs. At this point, me being a scrupulously honest narrator almost all of the time, I'll have to confess to a bizarre urge which came over me. I came close to asking my brother in arms to grab my phone from my jacket pocket and take a snap of me with the lad clinging to my back, but fortunately common sense prevailed, by the skin of its teeth, so I was spared the looks of consternation and/or contempt that I'd have received for my sins.

I think I managed about half a mile before my shoulders slumped and my legs turned to jelly, so the lad obligingly released his grip and we had another rest. He then walked for a while and I believe the proliferation of buildings and brighter lights perked him up, so by the time we had to leave the beach he'd just taken one more short ride on his compatriot's back and walked the rest of the way.

At the foot of some steps we sat down and I urged him to eat and drink, because we were going to have to walk through the streets and couldn't risk drawing attention to ourselves. It was about half past five and there were already a few vehicles around, so I strove to convey that we'd have to look like three regular guys on their way to work. I also finally remembered to introduce myself.

"Hola, Richie. Yo soy Abdou," said the tireless young man with muscles of steel.

"Je suis Demba," the other lad murmured.

Abdou gently squeezed the back of his neck. "En español. *Yo soy* Abdou.

"Yo soy Ab... yo soy Demba," he said, smiling weakly.

Abdou then said a few unintelligible words of encouragement to him in French, before asking me what had become of the old Englishman.

I said that the police may have picked him up, but that he was a clever man and would know what to do.

"Is he your father?" Demba asked me in French.

"No, no es mi padre," I said in clear Spanish. "Peter es un buen amigo. Un hombre muy bueno. Ahora vamos a su casa."

After I'd checked that the coast was clear, we crossed the main road and headed along a deserted street parallel with Peter's. Despite the absence of traffic, I took a leaf out of his book and kept up a constant stream of chatter, interspersed with a few questions. Abdou was twenty-two and had lived in Dakar all his life. He'd worked as a fisherman on one of the many traditional boats and had been putting money aside for this trip for as long as he could remember. With his help I ascertained that Demba was just eighteen and hailed from a smaller city called Thies. He'd helped his father and brothers in their car repair garage, and it was they who had financed his voyage to Spain, where he was to join two cousins in Barcelona.

"And who do you know in Spain?" I asked Abdou as the house came into view.

"Oh, I have friends in Madrid, but I don't want to stay there."

"Hmm, no, there are many Senegalese in Madrid."

"Sí, muchos." He squeezed Demba's neck again. "Maybe I go with my new friend to Barcelona. Qu'est-ce que tu dis, Demba? Dois-je aller à Barcelone avec toi?"

He smiled. "Oui, oui, viens avec moi à Barcelone."

I smiled and nodded. "Una buena idea."

The constructive nature of this final leg of our journey almost made up for the fact that there was no sign of Peter's car, so I assured them that he'd be returning soon, before we stealthily entered the house, kicked off our damp shoes, and entered the kitchen. After nipping upstairs for Peter's dressing gown and another that he'd lent me, I told them to strip off and put them on, before asking them if they wished to eat something before they bathed. By now they were both ravenous, but when I grabbed a large pack of bacon from the fridge Abdou pointed out that they were Muslims, so I set about making a six-egg tuna omelette instead, after inviting them to help themselves to milk and cereals.

I'd put the washing machine on and was in the process of slicing and buttering two large baguettes when I heard a car pull up outside. As I watched Peter approach the door, casually twirling his keys, I had a feeling that he'd bested the civil guards in one way or another. This proved to be the case, because after introductions had been made and we'd all tucked into our breakfast, he told me that he'd followed my suggestion and made his way through the campsite to the road, where he'd managed to climb over the wall.

"I was just about to turn up the track to the car when a civil guard jeep came flying along and screeched to a halt in front of me. I kept my cool and when the young officers ordered me into the back of the jeep it occurred to me to launch into an irate speech in English. I'd have been hesitant in my lousy Spanish, you see, and I wanted to gain the upper hand and stop them bossing me around. They didn't understand a word, of course, so when I'd done and they were looking a bit perplexed, I said in Spanish that I'd just walked along the beach from town to pick up my car, which I'd left up the track after drinking too much to drive in the restaurant yesterday. I asked them if there was any law against an insomniac walking at night and pointed along the track to my car, so we walked up and they told me to open it. After they'd shone their torches inside and in the boot, I think one of them was ready to let me go, as he'd just muttered to his mate that they'd be finishing their shift soon, but the other guy was a bit more officious and accused me of helping Africans to get away from the beach.

"I looked astonished, then burst out laughing. Why would I want to help a lot of bloody negro scum? I said to them, before ranting on that I wished their damned pateras would all sink so they'd stay in their shithole of a country, and stuff like that. I thought I might get the typical racist response to this tirade, but they both seemed shocked and looked at each other as if they thought I had a screw loose. The officious one wanted to take me in the jeep, so I complained that I wasn't some filthy immigrant who they could order around, but that I'd be happy to drive back to the barracks if their superiors wanted to question me."

He chuckled and shook his head. "I was making it up as I went along, surprised by how much I could say in the heat of the moment. Then I said that I'd always wanted to go inside the barracks to see how my favourite police force operated, before telling them that I'd preferred Spain when Franco was alive, because he'd known how to deal with blacks, commies, queers and other degenerates. By then they really thought I was nuts, but the bossy one was a bit nervous about not taking anyone back, because of course the useless sods hadn't picked up any of the others, or at least that's the impression I'd got.

"Anyway, the nicer one came with me in the car and I did get to see right inside the barracks, but I had to wait until six when their superior started work. I was sat in a scruffy office and I could hear the stroppy one droning on to him, then when this older bloke with a big moustache came in, I stood to attention and gave him my best fascist salute."

Peter showed us what he'd done and looked very funny indeed with his face set in a passionate, almost manic expression.

"So what happened then?"

"Well, I was going to say Viva Franco or even Heil Hitler, but he gave me such a withering look that I lowered my arm and just saluted the photo of the king on the wall. 'Get this lunatic out of here and make me some coffee,' he hollered, and here I am, safe and sound, more torturer than tortured, I think."

I looked at the lads and pointed to the man of the moment. "Todo bien con mi amigo."

"No problemas con policia?" Abdou asked Peter.

"No, no hay problemas."

"But might the guards not ask around and find out that you're actually a perfectly sane and lovely man?"

"Hmm, I dunno. Maybe it'll get back in a garbled form to the blokes who're suspicious about what I've been getting up to. It might soon be time for me to visit the Betis bar and test the water there. Right, let's get these lads in the shower then off to bed. How've they been?"

I told him that Abdou was as strong as an ox, and that Demba was now looking remarkably well, considering his debilitated state during their long march to safety.

Peter topped up Demba's water glass and observed him closely. "Probably just a lack of energy after spewing up so much and getting cold. I don't think he's dehydrated, but we'll keep him here for at least two days, just in case. Not long after I started doing this an older man insisted on moving on quickly from one of our colleague's houses and died soon after in Madrid, of a heart attack, his nephew told Juanjo, the chap they'd stayed with, so we've been more careful since then."

"I'll run a hot bath for Demba."

"No, quick showers and off to bed with them both."

We soon accompanied them upstairs and left them to it in the bathroom, before Peter rattled his keyring and smiled.

"This is the moment you've been waiting for, though not in the circumstances I'd have chosen."

I held my breath as he opened the door of the fourth bedroom and flicked on the light.

"Now you won't have to keep trying the door."

"Ah, well... ooh, they're big lights," I said as I inspected two large umbrella-shaped lamps.

"Softboxes, and that square one's an LED panel light." He pulled a brown textured screen down from its cylindrical casing. "I've got three backdrops, but this is the one I've used the most." He pushed away a chair and tapped on the door of a heavy old wardrobe. "The rest of my gear's locked in here, but there'll be time enough to look at that. Give me a hand with this."

We soon opened a two-seater sofa bed and Peter went to fetch the bedding from a drawer in my room. I sat on the upright chair in front of the screen and imagined him taking my portrait. He found me with my head tilted back, staring into an imaginary camera.

"You look like Napoleon on his throne. I can see it'd be hard work to get you to pose naturally."

"Who've you photographed in the last four years then?"

"I started with that farmer's family, then I did a few of my kids and grandkids when they came over, but I didn't really get inspired till I saw a young woman working in a restaurant who I liked the look of."

I pricked up my already responsive ears. "Ah, a woman, right."

He smiled. "Twenty-eight years old and not interested in a grandpa like me, but I could somehow see her face in a Vermeer painting. Not Girl with a Pearl Earring exactly, but... anyhow, I bought a darker screen and one of those softboxes, then practiced on Denise when she was here. I showed those photos to the lass and she agreed to come and pose. I was pleased with the results, and so was she, so since then I've been inviting people whose faces truly interest me to come and be photographed."

I raised my chin again.

"Yours doesn't, I'm afraid, but I'll satisfy your vanity one of these days." He blew some dust from the top of a tripod and yawned.

"Have you photographed any of the Senegalese lads?"

"Just three of them. The racist persona I played earlier would have said that all black faces look alike, but that's not true at all, even though many Senegalese men might strike us Europeans as similar looking. Oumar's face didn't interest me, for instance, but I did photograph Cheikh. I don't have a decent printer, so I later emailed him the files and he was chuffed to bits."

"Why don't you have a decent printer?"

He shrugged. "You've seen the pictures on my walls, all by well-known artists. I don't especially like to see my own work all the time. I've digitalised quite a lot of prints and I can look at my stuff on the computer with the big monitor in my study if I feel like it, but... well, I believe many writers hate to reread their own books, so I guess it's the same sort of thing with my photos. When I was a working photographer I just had to come up with the goods, while now it's the process of portraiture that I enjoy."

"Do you find Demba and Abdou's faces interesting?"

He sighed. "I should have made you sleep downstairs, after all."

"Well? Final question."

"Oh, I don't know yet. Maybe Abdou's."

"And he's built like an Olympic gymnast. You could photograph him from the waist up. Did I tell you that he carried Demba for ages? I did for a while too, but–"

"Richie, please stop. It's seven o'clock."

"I don't feel sleepy at all."

"You will. Now go and hang that washing out in the patio while I show them to their rooms."

"All right. Thanks for showing me this one."

"I hope I don't live to regret it."

8 – An Idle Interlude

A few nights later a helicopter with powerful searchlights was spotted flying up and down the coast. The following day two SEMAR patrol boats cruised around some way out to sea, putting on a spurt now and then for no apparent reason.

"I believe they're doing that for our benefit," Peter said as we sat on a bench on the seafront, resting in the mild sunshine after a heavy lunch.

I looked around at the Sunday trippers who had flocked to Chipiona on that lovely autumn day. "Hmm, maybe."

"Not so much for these people as for us. Me and you and the rest of our group. Perhaps they hope we'll tell the people smugglers not to come here again."

I felt a swell of pride. I'd already been congratulated by Elise for leading the two lads to safety all the way along the beach, and she'd spread the word via text messages that Richie from England was a great asset to the team. This had occurred when we thought we'd completely foiled the Guardia Civil by managing to give their three jeeps the slip on that memorable night, but Peter had gleaned from a well-connected gossip in the Betis bar that after the six guards had received a severe bollocking for messing up so badly, the

Benemérita – or Meritorious, as the Civil Guard likes to call itself – had summoned its finest brains and begun to investigate.

Peter and I suspected that they'd managed to intercept and decipher some of Elise's texts, because – she'd told us from a different phone – officers had been questioning her neighbours but had yet to knock on her door, so she feared that the net was closing in.

"I believe she's told the smuggler who she's in touch with not to come here for a while, but as he's probably just a minion, it won't necessarily stop them. The bosses couldn't care less if the passengers get caught, as they've already paid their fares, though of course they don't want to lose their precious pateras. My guess is that they'll bide their time for a while, then they might send one of their oldest boats to test the water, but this is pure speculation."

I sighed the sigh of the hero in repose, enjoying his downtime but already itching to get back into action. Abdou and Demba had proved to be good company, appreciative of our ministrations and content to remain indoors until we felt sure that the younger man had recovered completely. By the time we drove them to Seville on the third day after their arrival, they'd become firm friends and were both going to try their luck in Catalonia. It turned out that Demba's cousins were in fact living in Sabadell, a large town a few miles inland from Barcelona, where they'd found unofficial but not badly paid work in a large distribution hub. Although Abdou's friends were awaiting him in Madrid, he'd agreed that it would be preferable to avoid meeting up with them, lest they convince him to stay and share their hand-to-mouth, blanket-toting existence, so Peter had plotted a bus route by way of Granada to Murcia, then up the coast to Spain's most prosperous region.

After they'd gone I tried to settle down to my studies, but the grammar books seemed ever so boring after all the interesting conversations we'd had, so I selected a Spanish translation of Walter Scott's Ivanhoe from Peter's bookshelves and began to struggle through it, seeing many parallels between that brave knight's trials and tribulations and my own future brushes with authority. Once I'd put the book down, however, I generally felt content to rest on the laurels of the one selfless and moderately brave deed I'd performed in my whole life, unless you count the time I'd dragged a skinny lad to safety after he'd gone under during a personal survival session in the local swimming pool when I was about ten.

Back to that heartfelt sigh. "Ah, I expect it'll all blow over soon and we'll be back in business."

Peter sniggered. "Oh, boy, all that praise has really gone to your head."

"Not at all." I uncrossed my legs, as real men sit with both feet on the ground. "But you said it would give me a buzz and it certainly has. Hanging out with the people we've helped is great too, then they go, and... well, everything seems a bit boring afterwards."

"I know what you mean, but that close shave has finally convinced me that it's time for me to pack it in. A younger man would have been over that campsite wall in a flash and back in the car before those guards arrived, but I'm just too old to be getting up to that sort of thing. Being deported is a real danger too, as Elise may be about to find out, and after making a life for myself here I'm becoming unwilling to take that risk. No, I'm going to do one final pickup, assuming we have any more, then call it a day."

This last phrase dispelled my feeling of disappointment more than I'd anticipated, as the mention of deportation had struck a disturbing chord. If I were expelled, I'd end up back in my mother's house, and neither she nor anybody else, with the exception of Denise, would believe I'd done anything other than balls things up yet again. Carrying an African along a beach in the dead of night? Pull the other one, Idle Rich! Besides, I'd soon be back at the Job Centre, glowering into John's beady eyes, before he printed off an agency job at a warehouse on some godforsaken industrial estate and told me to get myself there – without a car – and be interviewed for a post I couldn't fail to get, as they'd be crying out for desperate deadbeats like me...

"Yes, all things considered, I think I'd like to do it just one more time too."

"I'll tell Elise, or whoever takes over from her. Some of our team will carry on regardless, you know, even if they have to drive for miles to reach a boat. It's become something of an obsession with them, almost like a drug. Most of them are well enough off, but golf, travel or whatever just don't satisfy them, so they do this as well. As with me, it'll be old age that finally makes them give it up." He patted my hand. "Yes, we'll do one more, knowing that it's the last time, then... then what?"

"You can go on enjoying your retirement and try to stoke up some interest in your photography."

"Hmm."

"I think you're really talented. Some of your old photos are brilliant, as well as the recent portraits. You should have persuaded Abdou to sit for you."

"He seemed reluctant, so I didn't persist. The subject's attitude is crucial."

I raised my chin.

"He or she must be willing, but not driven by vanity like you are. To interest me their face must seem to tell a story, like the Migrant Mother picture on the wall in my study," he said, referring to a famous photograph taken by Dorothea Lange during the Great Depression (which you'll find easily enough online). "Her careworn face, with that mixture of resignation and stubbornness in her eyes, tells us as much about the suffering they went through as Steinbeck's Grapes of Wrath. My best portrait of Cheikh is as close as I've come to that masterpiece so far, but it's a trifling snap in comparison."

"No, it's a wonderful picture. For me it sums up the migrant experience. There's hope and stubbornness in his eyes, with a trace of... wistfulness."

"Bullshit. You're just reading into it what you've seen in the other lads."

"A lot of discerning people would appreciate it too. If you put it online, in the right place, I bet thousands would see it and share it."

"Pah, online! There's no way I'm going down that road at my time of life. I do occasionally look at stuff on Flickr and Instagram, but even the best photographers post mostly mediocre and overprocessed images. No, photography's a very personal thing for me nowadays. I may never equal that portrait of Cheikh, but it won't be for... it won't be easy."

I lightly punched his thigh. "It won't be for want of trying, you were going to say. Now that *is* bullshit, because you're not trying at all."

"Oh, do you think Leonardo da Vinci saw birds like Lisa del Giocondo every day of the week?"

"Who?"

"The Mona Lisa, idiot."

"Yes, well, he painted lots of women when he was struggling for money, and he just happened to get that one right, though for all we know he might have prettified her. The point is that you enjoy dragging me up those lighthouse steps three times a week more than doing something you're genuinely good at."

"I'm good at that. If there's an over-seventies category in the race they're planning to do, I'll walk away with the gold medal."

"Big deal. Look there, at that old fella, the one with the stick. His face tells a story, doesn't it?"

"Hmm, yes. He's a retired bank cashier from Seville whose children are doing well. He's satisfied with his life, on the whole, but suffers from pangs of regret for not having struck out alone and tried to make something of himself. The arched eyebrows and somewhat self-satisfied expression suggest that he supports Seville rather than Betis, Seville being seen as the posher team, but, alas, he can no longer afford a season ticket."

"I think he's a retired... tobacconist, with a gambling addiction that he's been almost cured of."

Peter laughed. "The good thing about a portrait is that the viewer can read into it what they will, a bit like how the reader sometimes finds himself in a book."

I sighed. "Yes, I thought I was Ivanhoe for a while, and back in England I was like a… feckless chump in some crappy sitcom."

"And who'll you be next?"

"Well, the Ivanhoe fantasy was an idle daydream that distracted me from the fact that I've got to find a job at some point."

With a revolving finger and suitable sound effects, Peter produced the scratched record simile for me.

"Yeah, I know. Ooh, look at that little girl with the plastic hoop. She's got a timeless sort of face. You take her to the country, dress her in old-fashioned clothes, give her a wooden hoop, and you've got yourself a classic portrait."

Peter grasped my elbow and pushed it up. "Yes, go and propose to that muscle-bound dad of her that he lend us his daughter for the day and see what he says, or does."

"Yes, well, at least I'm being observant, unlike you."

"There's no point getting interested in people who you can't possibly approach. They have to live here for one thing. I keep my eyes peeled around the shops and bars, thus the portrait of Maribel."

"That's another cracker of a picture. Not as good as Cheikh, in my opinion, but still excellent."

He chuckled. "I took a few and that's the one she liked the least. She told me she had another printed, where she was pouting at the camera, but I caught her off guard in the good one."

"And immortalised her forever, on your computer."

"I'll leave you my files in my will." He patted his belly and yawned. "Listen, after our well-deserved nap, I'll finally open the cupboard and you can choose a camera to use, as you seem keener than I am."

I rubbed my hands together. "Oh, goodie. I'll probably be pretty useless, but I might inspire you to get your finger out and fulfil your true vocation."

"Hmm, that reminds me. Weren't you going to start writing some stories? Maybe that'll be your true vocation."

I stood up. "Not enough material yet. Come on, let's get this siesta over with."

He yawn-groaned as he pushed himself to his feet.

9 – Camera Chatter

"Only daft hipsters and a few true traditionalists shoot with film these days," Peter told me as I feasted my eyes on his collection of mostly old cameras and lenses.

"The Hasselblad's super-cool, and this Rolleiflex too. The broken Leica and the Contax are a bit titchy, but they all simply *ooze* nostalgia."

"Oh, God, I fear you're about to be bitten by an expensive and ultimately pointless bug. Look, these two big ones only take twelve frames per roll. The film, if you can find it, costs a packet, then all they do in the modern labs is develop the negatives and digitalise them. Some folk still shoot in black and white and do all the processing in their own darkroom, but I can tell you now that it's not going to happen here. I had my fill of that in my early days, stinking out the whole house. Look at this one."

I stroked the chrome on the Rolleiflex while turning up my nose at the boring Canon camera he was showing me.

"This is the DSLR I use for my portraits with the 90mm lens. I've also got this cheapish zoom lens for it." He deftly attached it to the camera body. "This'll be better for you to have a go with, as it gives you more options."

"Oh, I wouldn't want to risk damaging your main photographic tool."

"Just remember to keep the strap around your neck. It's built like a brick anyway, and it's not worth that much, as in four years it's become almost obsolete in most modern photographers' eyes. They have to have the latest and greatest with so many zillion pixels, astounding autofocus, and a load of other bells and whistles, but it still meets my needs perfectly."

I picked it up and frowned. "It's a bit heavy to cart around."

"Not much heavier than the Rolleiflex and the Hasselblad."

"No, but I bet they'd be real conversation-starters, while this black thing is just a… big electronic lump. Anyway, if we go out and I use this, what will you use?"

He smiled. "I'll just watch you and give you a few tips, if you like."

I tutted like a Scottish schoolmarm. "Oh, no you don't. I want to watch an old master in action, slinking through the crowd like a panther, then 'click', another amazing image."

"I've never been keen on street photography, if that's what you mean, though a lot of youngsters seem to enjoy it these days. In Spain you're not allowed to take photos of strangers though, unlike in Britain, so they have to be a bit stealthy. You see them in action in the cities, which reminds me that it's about time we took a trip somewhere."

"Yes, I'd like that. We could go to Seville and see the Giralda and all that."

He wrinkled his nose. "If you like, but there's a more photogenic city I'd like to take you to first, and it's nearer." He smiled. "I enjoy photographing water, and there's plenty of that there."

"Cádiz?"

"Right first time." He began to root around in the wardrobe. "Ah, yes, this'll do me just fine."

"It looks like a right cheap little thing."

He wiped some dust from the small red camera. "It's a point and shoot that I picked up at a flea market back home to replace the one that got pinched. Six megapixels and you can't see a damned thing on the screen when it's sunny. Still, it's not bad for ten quid. Now where's the charging cable…"

As I fondled the big Canon I began to like it more. It had a chunky grip to hold onto and with the smallish zoom extended it certainly looked like a serious piece of kit. Still, etiquette demanded that I say the right thing.

"I guess I'll use that little one, while you show me how it's done with a proper camera."

"Oh, no. I'll use the compact and we'll see who gets the best photos. If nothing else, it might show you that vision is far more important than equipment, unless you're a born photographer."

"You know, it's pathetic how few photos I've taken over the years. At weddings and whatnot, and whenever I travelled anywhere, I was usually too idle to put a film in the little Kodak my parents gave me, always leaving it up to others to record things for posterity. My entire photograph collection's in a folder at my mother's and I doubt there are more than a hundred snaps, many of me as a youngster. Sad, really."

Peter squeezed my shoulder. "In a while when the light's good we'll go out for a little photo walk. Who knows, it might be the beginning of a great adventure."

I raised the Canon's viewfinder to my eye and pressed the unresponsive shutter. "I hope so."

He flicked open a flap and slipped out the battery, before rooting around for the charger.

"You said we'd come out when the light was good, but there's hardly any left," I moaned on the seafront as the hazy sun neared the horizon.

"This is the golden hour, every serious photographer's favourite time, though it doesn't last long."

"An hour, presumably."

"More like twenty minutes in reality."

"I guess we might get a decent sunset."

I believe he turned a scoff into a light cough. "I'll leave that to you, while I use the light more constructively." He held his titchy camera at arm's length and aimed it at an empty bench. "Nice light, but still a bit too bright. Let's walk down to that wooden watchtower on the beach."

"Wouldn't the port be better, with all those lovely boats?"

"Later. There's too much visual information for you there now."

I took a shot of the coastguard's tower, then I made for a colourful kiddies' slide and snapped that. I turned to see Peter still circling the tower without raising his camera, so I plodded back to see what was keeping him. He told me that whenever he found something of interest he liked to study the scene thoroughly before deciding how to photograph it.

"It's just a wooden tower, though I suppose I could shoot the sunset through it."

"That'll be a hit on Instagram." He sighed. "Sorry, the last thing I want to do is get snobbish about photography. I'll just let you do your own thing." He went on circling the tower, backing off and closing in, stretching here and crouching there, with his hand clamped firmly around the camera.

"So what's your thing right now, Peter?"

"Just looking at the light and shadows from every angle, trying to anticipate the right moment to take a shot. With digital I like to pretend I'm using a film camera, paying for every exposure. It makes me more disciplined. Besides, it's a real bore to go through a load of poor shots on the computer, deleting them all." He looked at the Canon hanging inertly from my neck. "Then again, a talented American called Garry Winogrand was quoted as saying that he photographed to find out what something would look like photographed."

"Meaning?"

"Meaning that you might be as well to just shoot whatever you like, then see what you've taken later. You should get at least a thousand shots from that battery, and you'll need practice to get the exposure right, so don't mind me, just fire away to your heart's content. The great Cartier-Bresson once said that your first ten thousand photos are your worst, so you might as well get them out of the way sooner rather than later. Mind you, in his day that meant shooting and developing about... three hundred films, which isn't quite the same thing."

"I'll take a few more then," I said, pleased to hear the enthusiasm in his voice, as my purported reason for getting him out was to try to reactivate his creativity. It seemed a shame that he was using such an inferior tool, however, so I decided to buy myself a camera quite soon, because even if I didn't prove to be a born photographer, I still ought to start recording my daily life now that it had become far more interesting than before. I recalled my urge to ask Abdou to photograph me and Demba on the beach. Was that just vanity, or a true desire to immortalise the moment? Vanity, I concluded, before beginning to follow Peter around the tower, trying to see what on earth he was looking for.

He rambled on about light, shadow, form and texture for a while, but when I saw the sun's lower edge reach the sea I simply had to trot towards the shore and fire off twenty or thirty shots, many of which looked fine on the camera's LCD screen. I returned to find Peter finally photographing a white wooden plank on the watchtower.

"That's just a wooden plank," I pointed out.

"Just a minute." He aimed and fired again, before switching off and pocketing the camera. "That's me done. Did you get your sunset shots?"

"Yes, some of the finest ever taken."

"Right, now the sun's gone it's what we call the blue hour, which can last up to an hour, so we might as well nip over to the port and see if you can do something interesting with the lights there."

The trouble with DSLR cameras, which were beginning to be superseded by mirrorless ones, is that you see the actual scene through the optical viewfinder, then often get something quite different on the screen. My first shots at the port came out way too dark, then I produced a few that were blisteringly bright, so Peter patiently explained a lot of stuff about aperture, shutter speed and exposure, before taking a pleasingly atmospheric shot of a fishing boat. He then pointed out that the camera was actually fairly idiot-proof, because by flicking a switch it was possible to see a live view of the scene on the screen, so I was able to use the remaining light to good effect and take a couple of photos that later pleased me on the computer monitor, unlike the sunset shots which were indeed predictably boring.

Now, not long after taking up photography I began to realise that most people's eyes tend to glaze over as soon as you begin to blather on about anything remotely technical, so in order not to lose my remaining readers I've decided to knock that sort of thing on the head right away and try to limit our photographic chatter to the bare essentials from now on. Back at the house, Peter processed the best of his three white plank shots, which actually included a blue plank and some rusty nails, before explaining that the play of light on what was essentially an abstract composition interested him more than fishing boats and whatnot. In my case, however, he reiterated that I ought to use my first ten thousand shots to photograph anything that took my fancy, in order to enjoy the learning process and improve my skills.

I really picked his brains that evening until he shut me up by thrusting a couple of photography books into my hands and telling me to read them from cover to cover.

I flicked through one weighty tome. "But there's no mention of digital photography."

"Chemical or digital, it makes little difference. It's the *art* of photography you have to learn about. Tomorrow we'll go to Cádiz and see if we can capture its essence."

"Great."

"At least this has taken your mind off finding a job."

I tore my eyes away from a gorgeous black and white picture of Venice. "A what? Oh, I won't be needing one of those for a while." I leaned over and peered into his eyes. "Hmm, definitely overtired. I fear it'll take some time to cure you of your exercise addiction."

We enjoyed a conspiratorial cackle, before I began to pen an overdue email to my paymasters.

10 – An Encounter in Cádiz

Cádiz, one of the oldest cities in Western Europe, was founded by the Phoenicians as a strategically placed trading post in a large bay. Nowadays a strip of land plus two bridges take the roads and railway to the island which is jam-packed with buildings, though the northernmost part of the city is the oldest and most interesting, housing a brace of cathedrals and umpteen churches, convents, palaces and so on, none of which you'll read much about here. Peter and I initially stuck to the coast which we followed all the way round from a huge, ornate cathedral to the no longer so ancient port that launched hundreds of ships to the New World, carrying a heady mixture of European religion, culture, greed and disease.

I felt a bit grumpy at first, because no matter how good the morning light was going to be, I still resented being awoken at six o'clock with the words, 'If you want to be a proper photographer, you'll have to get used to rising before dawn, sunshine.'

"It's still bloody dark," I moaned as we strolled along the seafront, vaguely discerning the waves crashing into the rocks below the wall.

Peter rubbed his chilly hands together. "The blue hour's about to commence."

"More like the black hour."

"By the time we've finished, all the so-called photographers will start to arrive with their posh cameras to take the same bright, boring old shots. I bet if we see another photographer now, he or she will be carrying one of these."

"I still can't believe you're going to put that daft little camera on a tripod. Folk'll laugh at you."

"Let them."

"Please use the Canon."

"Nope, I have a point to prove, mainly to stop you wasting a load of your... my son's money on an expensive camera," he said, as during the forty-minute drive, despite my fatigue, I'd been droning on about the cameras I'd been ogling on my new phone after turning in for the night.

"I'll get something cheap...ish." I felt the strap tugging on my neck. "And lighter than this."

We plodded on past some uninspiring modern flats, before rounding a bend and reaching a little beach from which a dimly lit causeway seemed to disappear into the sea. At the end of it, Peter assured me, there was an eighteenth-century fortress which would almost certainly be closed to the public.

"So why are we traipsing along here in this nasty wind?"

"I'm going to photograph Cádiz as the first rays of sun illuminate it."

After a couple of hundred yards I turned to see the city looking prettily lit up, so I extended my zoom and took a few photos. As the sky lightened, the scene only improved in my eyes, so as I trailed after Peter I kept stopping to fire off more inspired shots until I caught up with him on some rocks near the locked castle gates. The little red camera did indeed look silly screwed onto the professional tripod, but Peter insisted that a long exposure would mitigate the shortcomings of the tiny sensor and he hoped to capture an image fit to grace the pages of a travel magazine.

"I'm doing this mostly for your benefit, Richie, so pay attention."

"To what? We're just standing here getting cold."

"Patience is the key to good photography."

By way of reply I moved away and began to snap him from different angles and at different settings, confident that the law of averages would assure me of at least a couple of competent photos. I then turned my attention to the city and photographed it at least once a minute for the next half hour, while the maestro took a total of three long-exposure shots before declaring himself satisfied with his work.

"From a photographic point of view I'd be content to go home now, but I'd better show you around the city."

"It's not even nine o'clock and I'm just warming up, literally and artistically."

"Ah, you remind me of my early days, when I spent an arm and a leg on film for my Contax, shooting away at everything in sight. I guess the early stages of a photographer's journey are the most fun, when everything seems worthy of attention."

I took a shot of his tanned, smiling face, framed by the low fortress wall, then spotted an incoming fishing boat and snapped that too. In the next hour or so as we rounded the peninsula past another old castle and through a verdant park, I allowed my creative instinct to run riot, so by the time we reached the Baluarte de la Candelaria, a small fortress with great views across the bay to El Puerto de Santa María, I'd already completed 7% of my 10,000-shot apprenticeship – about 700 shots – and only 6% of battery power remained.

"Damn and blast it. I'm just getting going."

"Sorry, the battery must have weakened with age. Still, I wouldn't like to have to wade through all the rub... the photos you've taken, but I guess it's all part of the learning curve." He handed me the compact camera. "Now do your worst with this one."

So we shoved the trusty Canon into his rucksack and with the inconspicuous little camera in my hand I began to fire furtively at all the passers-by who interested me. After a bite to eat in a bar near the big container-filled port, I photographed a ship bound for the Canary Islands, before we finally headed into the bustling heart of the city. Peter had been right about the midmorning surge of photographers, because we began to spot them on every street, many of them using the digital rangefinder-style cameras which seemed to be in vogue. The black and silver devices with several shiny dials on top made my little red thing look like a piece of junk, and when a bearded young hipster-type shot me at close range then walked away sniggering, I slipped it into my pocket and declared that I was done for the day.

"Don't let that hairy poser put you off, Richie. Social media's making those cameras into a fashion statement and folk just like poncing around with them, a bit like they used to do with SLRs in the seventies. If you stay interested, I'll teach you what I know, but you can take it from me that almost any digital camera made in the last few years will be perfectly adequate for your needs."

"I really fancied getting one of those cool Fujifilm's too, but not any more," I moaned, before whipping out my cheapo tool and impulsively taking a selfie with Peter by my side.

I'm aware that I did promise not to drone on about photographic matters, but I think what happened next goes some way to justifying this chapter so far, because as I relaxed my grip on Peter's shoulder, an attractive lady strode boldly towards us.

"I thought I recognised you, Peter," the slim brunette said in Spanish.

"Hola, Lourdes. What brings you here?"

"Just a visit to the lawyer, I'm afraid."

"Ah, yes, you're a real Gaditana, aren't you?"

"Sí, born and bred here."

"This is my friend Richie from England. He's staying with me for a while."

I blushed as her lips brushed against each of my cheeks.

"Hola, Richie, encantada."

"Igualmente, Lourdes."

"Lourdes has been living in Chipiona for many years and works at the health centre," Peter told me in clear Spanish.

"Ah, bien."

"How old are your kids now?" he asked her, mainly for my information, he later told me.

"Alberto is seventeen and Rocío has just turned nineteen. She's studying in Seville now," she said to us both, as if she wished to assure me that they'd both passed the tiresome stage, I chose to believe.

That probably makes her at least forty, I mused, though she doesn't look a day over thirty-five…

"Are you here on holiday, Richie?"

"Eh? Oh, well… yes, but a long one. I mean… er…"

"Richie is seeing how life in Spain suits him, before deciding whether or not to stay," Peter intervened. "At home he's a librarian, not a job he can do here, so while he keeps me company he's beginning to look into possible opportunities."

Lourdes's smile revealed a far better set of teeth than my slightly yellowed gnashers, so I warned myself not to get my hopes up. Thus the shy glance I gave her, rather than the brash come-hither look of my younger days. Besides, she was no dowdy, dull-witted Lancashire lass, but a refined, well-dressed city girl who probably wouldn't give a second glance at a loser like me, not when she found out about my life of heroic underachievement.

"I see you already speak Spanish," she said.

"Sí, pero mal…amente."

"He's a fast learner," said my backer who seemed determined to paint me in the best possible light. "And a born teacher." His eyes narrowed. "You know about my guests from overseas, don't you, Lourdes?"

Her lovely brown eyes also narrowed. "Yes, I do."

"Well, Richie's been marvellous with three recent ones, teaching them Spanish and generally making them feel welcome."

Now the lady really beamed at me, suggesting that she thoroughly approved of the migrant business. I was dying to ask Peter all about her, but she seemed to be in no hurry to move on, so I shrewdly suggested that we all repair somewhere for coffee. As we made our way along a narrow street to a bar called Casa Lazo I brought up the rear, gazing at her glossy shoulder-length hair and willing her to wish to go to powder her nose. When my wish was granted, I hustled Peter over to a corner table and begged him to tell me all.

"What about?"

"About Lourdes, of course. I need to know how to approach her."

He sighed. "With caution, if I were you."

"Why's that? She isn't a nymphomaniac, is she?"

"I wouldn't know, but I do know that her ex-husband is a total pain in the arse. They got divorced a few years ago, but I believe he still won't leave her in peace. That's to say, if she hangs out with her girlfriends, he tends to let her be, but whenever she goes anywhere near a bloke, he suddenly becomes her shadow and makes her life a misery."

I tensed my right fist, then tried and failed to crack the knuckles. "What's he like?"

"Oh, a wiry sort of guy, not much taller than she is."

As this would make him at least four inches shorter than me, I said that I wouldn't let some pesky little shrimp put me off.

"He's strong though, being a fisherman."

I shrugged as I flicked a crumb from the table with my powerful index finger.

"And he's prone to violent outbursts."

I growled softly. "Did he beat Lourdes?"

"Oh, no, but he did once come to blows with another fisherman and broke his nose."

I chuckled nervously. "What, another midget like him?"

"No, a big fella, as tall as you, but broader."

"Ah."

"Who got annoyed by that punch and threw him into the harbour, much to everyone's amusement. He's just been a pest, really, making it hard for Lourdes to get on with her life, but I wouldn't let it worry you. Here she comes. Ah, Lourdes, do you still drink cortados?"

She surveyed us both with an amused gleam in her eyes. "Sí, por favor."

So Peter ordered two small coffees with milk, plus a manly café solo for me, before we lapsed into silence until I said the first thing that came into my head.

"Do you come here often, Lourdes? To Cádiz, I mean."

"Often on Sundays, to see my parents, but rarely midweek."

"Ah."

She looked at Peter. "My father and I have been talking to his lawyer about Miguel Ángel. We're going to see if the court will place some kind of restraining order on him."

"What's he been up to?"

"Oh, all sorts of annoying things. Thanks to him I've given up social media, which has turned out to be a blessing, but since I went out to dinner with a locum doctor he's been hanging around the health centre in the afternoons, half drunk and making a fool of himself. He's trying to turn our children against me too, but that only makes them despise him more. I've been reluctant to resort to the law, but it's been four years now and I'm sick and tired of his harassment. I mean, I do feel sorry for him and I wish he'd get his act together, but I have to think about myself too, don't you think?" she said, before calmly sprinkling some sugar into her coffee.

"Absolutely. Don't you agree, Richie?"

"Er, I have understood… something. Hmm, yes, the lawyer can be the best way, I think," I said gravely, cursing my inability to follow normal conversation, as Lourdes had provided me with no subtitles.

She smiled at me. "Enough about my little problems," she said more slowly. "What have you two been up to?"

"Oh, nothing special. We do a lot of exercise together," Peter said. "And we are now doing some photography. As I said, we have had three guests from overseas, but I fear that these visits will end soon."

"More boat patrols have been seen recently."

"Exactly."

"Perhaps you have done enough now. It is risky for you, and not everyone understands why you do it."

He chuckled. "I know. I am no longer the harmless old Englishman who everybody liked to talk to."

"I'm glad the man you brought to the health centre got away to Madrid without problems. How is he doing?"

"I didn't hear from him again. Anyway, today's lucky meeting reminds me that we no longer meet for coffee like we used to."

"No, it's a pity we haven't."

"Let's meet soon in Chipiona."

She noticed my instinctive nodding and smiled. "Do you still go to that campsite restaurant you took me to once, Peter?"

"Yes, Richie and I have been twice recently, once for lunch, and also a... flying visit we made."

Seeing those searchlights in my mind's eye reminded me of our valiant exploits and emboldened me to suggest meeting there for lunch at the weekend.

Her eyes twinkled delightfully and, I hoped, delightedly. "Yes, that's a good place for me. How about this Saturday?"

My eyes subtly perused her svelte body beneath her light jacket. "Yes, and perhaps we can go for a swim first."

She giggled charmingly (and to hell with those style snobs who disapprove of adverbs). "Oh, the water will be too cold for me, but you two can go ahead."

"We still swim most days," said Peter.

Not for long, I thought, as those plunges were becoming a tad chilly for me. "Yes, and we climb the lighthouse steps several times every week," I said, mainly because I knew how to.

She rubbed her flat stomach. "I should do more exercise. Right, I have to go."

On exchanging a second set of kisses I felt the moistness of her full red lips on my cheeks. After she'd walked enchantingly out of the bar I fell back into my seat, then slumped forward and hid my face in the crook of my arm.

"What's up with you, son?"

"Oh, it's at times like these that I curse my wasted life," I lamented histrionically. "Why am I not a doctor or a lawyer, so I can face a lady like Lourdes with my head held high?"

"Because you've been a lazy bastard since you were so high," he said as he patted my head.

"I'm not even a librarian. I'll have to set the record straight about that little white lie of yours."

"I wouldn't worry about a minor detail like that. What makes you think she's interested in you anyway?"

I finally stopped clowning around and raised my head. "Experience. If there's one thing I've got on my CV, it's plenty of women, so I can tell when one's keen."

He tutted like an empathic vicar. "Ah, but your experience of Spanish women is practically null, so there's something I ought to point out to you before you get carried away."

Peter went on to say that while women from northern climes tended to play hard to get but were sometimes apt to jump into bed at the drop of a hat, Spanish ladies were initially far more transparent in manifesting their feelings but, in his limited experience, their openness could be misleading.

"Oh, I've been meaning to ask you about women."

"What about them?"

"Well, about how you feel about them, for yourself, I mean?"

He gazed at me drolly. "If you're wondering if I've got over my wife's death, I'll have to say yes and no. No-one will ever replace my Mary, but that's not to say I'm not open to a little loving, should the opportunity arise. It did once, two summers ago, but she was a tourist from a town near Seville, so we passed like two old ships in the night and I haven't had any luck since then. Anyway, you'd better bear in mind that Lourdes's admiration for your stunning good looks and fabulous physique does *not* mean that she'll necessarily want anything more that platonic friendship, if that."

I felt the thin hair at the top of my increasingly noble brow, then ran my tongue over the teeth that I'd kept mostly under wraps in Lourdes's presence.

"All right, I'll try not to get my hopes up. I just got a bit excited about being so close to such a divine creature. How did you get to know her, anyway?"

It transpired that Peter and Lourdes had met at the health centre where she worked on reception soon after he'd arrived. They'd struck up a friendship that her husband must not have found threatening due to Peter's advanced age, and had met for a drink occasionally, both before and after her messy separation and divorce.

"You can imagine that I was delighted to knock around with such a lovely lass, and it was really good for my Spanish. I think she appreciated my objectivity, and as we had to speak in a simple way, we tried to find straightforward solutions to her problems. I liked to believe that I was the one who made her see sense and get out of her awful marriage, rather than letting it drag on any longer, but with the benefit of hindsight I guess I just played a small part. Of late we've seen less of each other, partly because of the migrant business taking up my time, but I also think she hasn't wanted to be seen with me, in case folk think she's involved too."

He sighed. "Yes, once I've called it a day I'll probably become a bit more popular again, because as well as the usual racists, there are some mildly conservative people who've chosen to steer clear of me, so they don't end up being tarred by the same brush. Only time will tell, but there are a couple of fair-weather friends I shan't even be giving the time of day to, because I know they've spread all sorts of rumours about me being a communist spy and other stupid stuff like that. In a way what I've said about Spanish women goes for the men here too. Whereas we Brits tend to be more reserved and even standoffish, you get talking to an Andaluz bloke and he's soon acting like you're his best mate, inviting you to his house and saying 'mi casa es tu casa' and crap like that. A few of them took me in at first, and it was good for my Spanish, but the fact is that some folk just want to make a foreign pal so they can show off to their real friends, so be warned."

"So have you not made any real friends here?"

"Just mates, and fewer than I thought. Come on, pay up and we'll be off."

As we made our way back towards the car I no longer paid much attention to my surroundings and even failed to take out the little camera in the crowded neoclassical market square. Peter pointed out that the people emerging from the shadows of the striking stone pillars were great photo opportunities, so I took a couple of half-hearted shots before asking him how old Lourdes was.

"Er, she'll have turned forty-one last month. It's the first birthday I've missed since we met."

I smiled dreamily. "So she married quite young then."

"Too young, she later realised. She was all set to go off to university in Seville when she met this dashing young fisherman at the carnival here. That's a colourful event that you might like to photograph in February."

"Yes, tell me more."

"Well there are floats and dancing and–"

"No, about Lourdes."

"Well, I think he whisked her off her feet and told her she was the girl of his dreams and all that. He boasted that he was going to add to his father's fleet of three fishing boats and tried to persuade her to drop everything and marry him. Her parents convinced her not to be too hasty, so she did begin her philology degree, but after about a year he managed to get her pregnant, so there was nothing else for it but to get married and move to Chipiona. Once the kids had started school, she got the job at the health centre and she's been there ever since."

"So she sacrificed her ambitions for that… drunken runt."

"He's actually quite an intelligent bloke and he sort of sacrificed his own ambitions to follow in his father's footsteps."

I pictured my own father climbing one of his many ladders. "And did he increase their fleet?"

"Did he heck. Fishing was on the wane by then and now he's only got one boat. He'll end up losing that if he doesn't get his act together. The hard drinking only started when Lourdes left him, so we shouldn't judge him too harshly. Oh, look at the play of light on the portico."

"Yeah." I held up the camera and clicked without looking at the screen, before asking him if Lourdes believed she'd wasted her life.

He grinned. "Like you think you've wasted yours, you mean?"

"Up to a point, yes."

"Well, unlike you, she's produced a pair of handsome children who I believe will do her proud, so she has no regrets on that score. Look, that German-looking guy has a digital Leica that must have cost him ten grand."

"Bully for him." I gazed sadly at the scratched screen of the titchy compact.

He slapped me on the back. "Come on, I know just the place where you can get yourself a nice little camera that won't cost the earth."

"I'm not thinking about that."

"Look, that's enough about Lourdes for now. You'll be seeing her on Saturday anyway."

I then opined that what she needed was an affluent partner who would enable her to pack in her dreary job and go back to university to fulfil her dreams. The doctor who she'd dated might be such a man, I said, but she'd be unlikely to wish to throw in her lot with a guy who could hardly speak the lingo and had zero job prospects.

"She quite likes her job and you've only just arrived. How the hell do you know what prospects you might have until you get out and meet people? Lourdes's fathe… oh, look at the gull on the bench. Set a fast shutter speed and see if you can catch it taking off."

"What were you going to say?"

"Something I'd have regretted." He grabbed the camera, fiddled with it, then began to close in on the sated bird, before tracking its take-off and pressing the shutter. "Bingo! Look at that."

"Nice."

"Maybe I've wasted my life too. I should have been a wildlife photographer, stalking leopards in the Serengeti, ha ha."

"What were you going to say about Lourdes's father?"

He gazed at me grimly. "Nothing important. Please drop it now and stop conjecturing about what may or may not happen. As things stand – and these are my very last words on the subject – I'd say you've got about a twenty percent chance of getting anywhere with Lourdes. Since she's been a free woman she hasn't opened her heart to any man, let alone her... anything else, so I don't see why you should have any better luck than her *many* other suitors."

"You don't know anything about that damned locum doctor," I grumbled. "I bet he earns a packet, whereas I–"

"Shut the f*ck up, Richie!"

As Peter rarely swore so vehemently I decided to keep my trap shut as he led the way back to the car. We were a sullen pair as he drove onto the mainland and few words were exchanged until we pulled into the carpark of a huge Carrefour hypermarket on the outskirts of the large town of El Puerto de Santa María. I assumed we were about to do a big boring food shop, but he led me through to the electrical department and the glitter of photographic gear soon perked me up. After inspecting some stonking great Nikons and Canons, then drooling over a lone black Leica rangefinder, I sniffed at the eye-catching Fujifilms that the posers used, before a smallish, reasonably priced Olympus caught my eye. It was black but had several shiny knobs on top and came with a retractable zoom lens that ought to fulfil my current needs.

"What do you think of this one?" I muttered.

"It's perfect for you. It's got a big enough sensor and great image stabilisation, plus a flippy screen that can be useful for getting high or low. You can buy other lenses for it if you want, but with the one it comes with you can slip it into a jacket pocket."

I recalled the research I'd done the previous evening. "Hmm, but a better model might come out soon."

"Oh, balls to that. Digital cameras have become so good that the manufacturers don't know what the hell to do next. The compact camera market has died a death and DSLRs are on the way out, so a nice mirrorless like that is just the thing for you." He put his hand under the rucksack which contained his Canon and pushed it up. "Hmm."

I smiled. "Heavy?"

He looked at the Olympus and nodded. "The Canon's good for my portrait work, but... no, I think I'll wait for you outside."

So Peter wandered off while I purchased the Olympus for a mere €649 – by far the cheapest of all the serious options – then he walked back in and got himself the silver and black version of the very same camera.

"This one will see me out," he said sheepishly as we headed for the car.

"I'm glad you've got one. We'll be able to learn all the settings together."

"Yes."

"And take them out on Saturday."

"Hmm."

"Don't you want to do a portrait of Lourdes?"

"No comment."

I peered into my bag at the shiny black box. "I think I do."

Later on we looked at the day's photos and the only ones of any real merit were Peter's long exposures of Cádiz which he'd shot with the titchy camera on the tripod. The best one of them could indeed have graced the pages of a travel magazine.

11 – A Decisive Day

On the migrant front, the SEMAR boat patrols had become a daily occurrence and we heard the sound of a helicopter almost every night. Elise had wisely decided to fly back to Belgium to spend some time with her family, so for the time being Søren the Danish doctor had become the main point of contact. The communicative smuggler believed that no pateras would be coming our way for the time being, so it seemed that the final pickup which Peter and I still wished to do wouldn't happen for a while. Søren understood why Peter wanted to pack it in, but a message he sent to him reiterated that my maiden effort had been appreciated. It went something like this:

It is a pity that R only wishes to do one more hike with us, as he is good company and the walking group needs energetic people like him.

So I felt flattered by that, and ever so pleased when Abdou called me from Sabadell to say that he and Demba were living with the latter's cousins and three of their friends. He told me it was a little crowded in the two-bedroom flat, but they all had mattresses and the building had a lift which he enjoyed very much. They hoped to begin work in the big warehouse before long, but this was dependent on a couple of people leaving, as the bosses had a quota of only so many undocumented workers, or that's what I understood. He even invited us to visit them, so I said we'd try to make it up there in the coming months, as Peter had suggested doing a tour to catch up with the guests with whom he'd remained in touch. These included Oumar, the first migrant I'd known, who after a period of silence had begun to text Peter again. After having a rough time in Madrid, trying to persuade his brother Idrissa to flee to Zaragoza with him, he'd eventually gone there alone and moved in with Moussa and his pals. He was yet to find a job, as the furniture factory wasn't overly busy, but he'd been making himself useful in the Senegalese community and had been assured that he'd soon be able to make some money one way or another.

Peter still intended to fly to Dakar sometime in the coming year, as he now had even more families to visit. I said that I'd like to join him, as long as it didn't make too much of a dent in the Contingency Fund which would soon be augmented by my redundancy payment. As return flights from Madrid could be had for as little as €500, he believed that I'd spend no more than a thousand altogether, as he intended to buy most of the presents and one could live very cheaply there.

As well as doing our usual exercise regime, including the lighthouse steps which I now climbed with ease, we spent a lot of time fiddling with and trying out our new twin cameras, so in one way and another the next three days passed by briskly enough. I didn't mention Lourdes more than thirty or forty times, though he still refused to talk about the lady whose lovely presence loomed large in my mind.

Finally the great day dawned and I had a lie-in while Peter went for a walk and a swim, as I wished to be in tiptop physical condition when we met Lourdes at one. The autumn weather was dreadful at home, my mum had told me on the phone, but on the Cádiz coast the sun shone warmly most days and the wind hadn't been too annoying, though I think I was getting used to it by then. As most of the local men had already ditched their shorts, I donned a pair of jeans and a smart short-sleeved shirt, as I didn't want to look like some lanky tourist who'd just stepped off the plane or motored down from Seville. With my soft brown shoes, a stylish pair of shades, and my cool new camera around my neck, I felt like quite a spruce dude as we waited at a table in the shade.

During the short drive to the restaurant Peter had brought his ban on speaking about Lourdes to an end. He'd solemnly advised me to try to relax and be myself, and under no circumstances to dwell on my chequered working life. I could mention the more respectable jobs I'd had – such as my spell in the office at the foundry and a longish stint as a hotel receptionist – if the subject arose, but I wasn't to harp on or even joke about all the menial posts I'd occupied, and I certainly mustn't remark on any of my many periods of unemployment. Instead I ought to highlight my studious nature and it would do me no harm at all to mention the hundreds of good books that I intended to have shipped over soon. When I lamented that it would all come out in the wash in the end, he said that first impressions were vitally important in any new relationship, and there'd be time enough to own up to my shortcomings should cupid's arrow hit the mark.

"You seem a lot more upbeat about my chances now," I said at the table as I gazed enviously at his ice-cold beer, a glass of which might have calmed my nerves, but given Lourdes's ex-husband's descent into heavy drinking, I'd decided to airbrush out my boozy past for the time being too.

He smiled. "I rate your chances more highly than I've admitted. I saw the way she looked at you in Cádiz, so unless you balls things up by demeaning yourself, I'm sure she'll be happy to go on a date with you."

"Well, you have changed your tune."

"Now's the time to buck you up, not three or four days ago."

"You're a master psychologist."

He shrugged, then perused me closely. "Take that cap off."

"You gave it to me."

"I know, but we're in the shade and you've put it on to hide your balding head."

"Receding hair, not balding head, if you please."

"Whatever, but let her see the real you."

I took it off and smoothed back my hair.

"Smile."

"Now?"

"Yes. No, not like a toothless granny. Bare your teeth. That's better."

"I must have used half a tube of whitening toothpaste in the last few days."

"You can tell," he lied.

Me and the master psychologist were presently joined by such a socially adept lady that I soon ceased to worry about what I should and shouldn't say, because Lourdes steered the conversation so ably that we were soon chatting away like old friends. Firstly she joked about how proud we seemed of our almost identical cameras, like two boys with their long-awaited Christmas gifts, making me laugh fit to burst and giving her a real eyeful of my teeth, fillings and all. Due to my still rudimentary Spanish which three days of intensive study had done little to improve, I was happy to listen to my friends reminiscing in an agreeably clear way about their previous meetings, without once mentioning her ex or any other irksome topic. In this way the meal passed pleasantly by, but I wasn't getting much of a look-in, so I decided that when the coffee arrived I'd begin to make my presence felt a little more.

Peter facilitated this by knocking back his cortado and declaring that he was off for a digestive stroll along the beach.

"Shall we…" I began, but he was already loping onto the sand, so I turned to face Lourdes and felt the blood rush to my face.

She smiled. "You have got a nice tan, Richie."

"Er, sí, I… Peter and I go out a lot, to walk and… things like that."

"Yes, you seem to be good friends."

"Yes, we are good friends."

"Tell me about the night you picked up the Senegalese men here."

"Well…" I pictured the scene and wondered how the hell I was going to describe such a fast-paced series of events without mangling the Spanish language so badly that she'd think me a congenital idiot, because it was one thing to come up with a coherent reply to a simple question, but quite another to embark on a lengthy narrative. I needn't have worried, however, because once I got started I realised that I'd been subconsciously rehearsing the tale ever since that fateful night. Words like searchlight, wasteland, barracks, fear, exhaustion and collapse tripped off my tongue with ease, and although my grammar must have left a lot to be desired, Lourdes's encouraging looks and nods enabled me to relate the whole adventure up to the point when Abdou, Demba and I tottered into the house.

"Home at last," Lourdes echoed, then chuckled. "A fascinating story, but you look tired now. Peter can tell me the rest."

"Ah, sí, gracias."

"Tell me one thing, Richie. When you speak, would you like me to correct you sometimes, or would you prefer me not to?"

Blush number two, and more intense than the first, because in those simple words Lourdes was effectively declaring her willingness to see more of me! While droning on about my exploits, a cluster of spare brain cells had been debating how best to go about inviting her out on a solo date, but I now ceased to worry about such a trifling matter, because Peter's rapid exit – and Lourdes's nonchalant acceptance of it – made me feel sure that we were going to have more opportunities to get to know each other. This was the first time in my life that a language barrier had hampered my usual smooth patter and I believed this to be no bad thing, because had I been able to wax lyrical in my usual fatuous way, she'd have taken me for the lackadaisical sort of bloke I'd been in almost all of my previous relationships.

Lourdes sported a plain white blouse and beige-coloured slacks, had her silky dark hair in a simple ponytail, and wore hardly any makeup or jewellery. Her smooth olive skin wasn't excessively tanned. She spoke articulately and didn't lisp quite as much as most local women, all of which made me believe she was a cut above the common herd in terms of class and culture. I could imagine her being a teacher – like my ex-long-term-girlfriend Julie, also quite a classy lady – or a medical professional rather than a mere health centre receptionist, and I'd just got to thinking about her family background when she asked me about my parents.

I spoke proudly of my solid working-class upbringing, omitted to mention that I'd failed to live up to my parents' expectations, then asked her about her own family. She was the youngest of three siblings and the only girl. One brother had married a girl from Granada and worked as a marketing manager there, while the other, also married, was an architect in Madrid.

"Ah, so you, the only daughter, and still living close to Cádiz, must be the apple of your parents' eyes."

"The apple? Oh, I understand. Here we just say child instead of apple."

When I blushed lightly she *squeezed* my hand and told me not to worry about making mistakes, because through trial and error I would come to master Castilian, as I clearly had a gift for languages.

"I think if you correct me, I will make better progress," I was bold enough to say, before looking round to see that my trim, tanned host had transformed himself into a mere dot, so far along the beach had he wandered.

"I will. Yes, I suppose I am the child of my parents' eyes, as my brothers only come home on holiday."

"What do your parents do? I mean, to what do they dedicate themselves?" I said, as I'd already learnt that our somewhat imprecise question isn't always understood in Spanish.

"My mother has worked as a dressmaker."

Oh, just a poor seamstress, I thought.

"While my father has been involved in a variety of enterprises."

At the mention of her father, my ears pricked up so abruptly that I swore I felt them move, because it had slipped my mind that Peter had been going to tell me about him in Cádiz, before thinking better of it.

"Ah, er… what kind of enterprises?

"Well, as he wasn't of a studious nature my grandfather gave him a little land, so he started out in agriculture, but later on he leased the land, much to his father's dismay, and began to import a variety of goods from China, something that not many people were doing at the time. He later branched out into property but got out of that before the 2008 crash. Since then he's just been indulging in his hobby, though still with an eye to making a profit, as he's always been a competitive character."

So is he stinking rich? I thought but didn't say.

"So has he been quite successful?" I couldn't help but ask.

"Yes, I suppose so, but I'm glad he's taking it easier these days, because he's sixty-eight and has suffered from poor health, mainly due to too many business lunches and not enough exercise, I believe." She turned to look at the dot on the beach which was becoming a bit bigger. "I've told him how fit my English friend is, despite being older than him, and he has improved his lifestyle a little, so his ulcers seem to have healed and he's lost some weight, though not enough."

"I'm glad… that he's healthier, I mean."

"Do you like cars?"

"Cars?"

"Yes, cars. You know, the things we drive around in."

Not especially, I thought, though I'd noticed that Lourdes had arrived in a shiny blue Audi A3 which must have been quite a stretch on her salary.

"Well, I… er…"

"Richie, please don't say what you think I want to hear. I'm sick of men who'll say or do anything to impress me."

I cleared my throat. "I have owned a rusty Mini, a… moribund Nissan Micra, and more recently an old but reliable Ford Fiesta. That's it, in my whole life."

She giggled. "Now I'll tell you what my father owns right now, as far as I know. In the garage under the flat in Cádiz he has a Volkswagen Golf which he shares with my mother."

"Ah, a nice car."

"And in his small industrial unit in El Puerto de Santa María he has three Porsches, two Ferraris, one Maserati, one Lamborghini, and a few cheaper cars like BMWs, Mercedes, and even a Jaguar that he says he can't sell for love nor money."

I gulped, nodded, then gulped again, because I had an inkling that she'd reeled off the list for a reason, and it wasn't to boast about her father's wealth, though a chap with a hobby like that must be up to his ears in money.

"I hope the unit has an alarm," seemed like a sensible thing to say.

"Oh, it's like Fort Knox, with a guard there around the clock." She smiled and shook her head. "The strange thing is that he doesn't especially enjoy driving those supercars. He likes to admire them – he even polishes them himself sometimes – and then make a good profit, before looking for another bargain."

I smiled. "So what is his modus operandi?"

"Very simple. Mostly through the property business contacts he made, he buys cars from wealthy people who are struggling and sells them to others who are prospering." Her gaze seemed to become momentarily shrewder. "Most of them are foreigners living on the Costa del Sol, but he prefers to keep his beloved cars closer to home."

"Ah."

This time her giggle seemed a tad less spontaneous. "The trouble is, his English is awful, so he sometimes has to hire an interpreter. He doesn't like to do this, as he fears that they might twist his words. He also complains that it takes away the fun to have a stranger involved."

"He should find a good assistant then. Like you, for instance."

"No, I don't wish to move in such circles. I don't like rich people much. They're so conceited, even if they try to hide it, and are generally far less interesting than they believe themselves to be. No, I prefer my job. It isn't too demanding and I enjoy chatting to all sorts of people. My salary is sufficient for my… for most of my needs, as my parents bought me a large flat when I got married, though it remained in their names until my divorce, as they never believed that Miguel Ángel and I would stay together."

Her divine brow clouded, then she turned to observe the figure on the beach whose limbs were coming into focus. She took her phone from her bag, prodded it a few times, then put it back. Lo and behold, Peter's form began to diminish once again.

She clasped her hands on the table and gazed at me solemnly. "I like you, Richie."

Blush. "Er, I like you too, Lourdes… mucho."

"So we like each other."

"That much is clear."

"For this reason I must tell you now that I'm not quite ready to have a relationship."

"Ah, well…"

"Listen, Richie, and I'll explain. If or when you and I do become more than friends, I don't want my ex-husband to spoil it by making a nuisance of himself. After leaving me alone for at least a year, he's been doing it again lately, just because I went for a perfectly innocent meal with a locum doctor who was sad to be stuck in Chipiona after his wife had given birth to their second child."

"You mentioned the doctor, and also a lawyer."

She sighed. "A restraining order is my father's idea, and his lawyers will know how to get one, but it really is a last resort for me." She clenched her ~~divine~~ fists, then wiggled her slender fingers. "Oh, if only I could convince Miguel Ángel to just get on with his life and leave me alone. He's a clever man, though you wouldn't know it right now, and still handsome too, though drinking has made him paunchy." She tapped her right temple. "I've a feeling that if only something would somehow click in his head, he'd see reason and realise that he's his own worst enemy and is making our children wish to avoid him."

As I couldn't come up with any ideas on the spot, I asked her if Peter had made any suggestions as to how to deal with him.

"When I last saw Peter, Miguel Ángel wasn't bothering me." She leaned towards me. "I believe your friend thinks I've been avoiding him because of his involvement with the migrants, but this isn't so. I've just become a bit less sociable of late, and as he was waiting for me to call… well, time has passed without us seeing each other."

I didn't know what she'd written in her quick text to Peter, but he had limbs again, so our private interview was drawing to a close.

"Peter and I will talk and think about your… Miguel Ángel and see if we can propose a solution," I said with an assurance I didn't feel, because short of getting her dad to pay someone to bump him off, nothing else had occurred to me so far.

She smiled. "Thank you. Perhaps men know better how other men think, but I haven't a clue what makes him behave so stupidly at such long intervals. Each time I think it will be the last, then he begins again, and it's been over four years now."

I then employed a mild manifestation of my tried and tested come-hither look. "Lourdes, I think it is in my interests to help your ex-husband to learn to forget you and get on with his life."

Her eyes sort of beckoned me thither in a similar way. "It is in both our interests, Richie. Look, here comes Peter."

"Right on time," I said, so he found us chuckling merrily away.

"Hola. Ah, that was good. I really needed to stretch the old legs," said the old man who'd walked three miles and swum in the ocean a few hours earlier.

"Richie and I have been talking about all kinds of things," Lourdes said, before summoning the young waiter.

"Yes, I expect you have."

We ordered more coffees and a bottle of water for the thirsty hiker.

"We've decided that you and he are going to put your heads together and try to find a way to combat Miguel Ángel's… misbehaviour."

Peter smiled. "I see. Is he still coming to the health centre in the afternoons?"

"Not since I showed him a photo of Felipe – that's the doctor – with his wife and their new baby, but… well, I hope the three of us will be getting together more often, so when he finds out that a handsome young man has joined the party, I fear that he'll start to get up to his old tricks as soon as he leaves the bar after work." She sniffed. "The smell of fish and alcohol annoy my colleagues, so I must avoid it at all costs."

Peter nodded. "Hmm, I suppose the simplest method might be for the handsome young man to simply throw him into the harbour again."

She took the liberty of feeling the handsome young fortysomething man's slender but not badly defined right bicep. "Better not, as lifting fish crates every day makes one very strong."

"Pah, I used to do judo." Anticipating the inevitable question, I admitted that I'd acquired my green belt about thirty years ago and hadn't stepped onto a mat since then.

"Violence rarely solves this kind of problem anyway," said Peter. "We must analyse the man's mind and try to come up with a constructive solution. Failing that, there's always the law court."

"I hope it won't be necessary, as it may make Rocío and especially Alberto lose their respect for him altogether."

I gasped and clicked my fingers. "That's it. The key to… his mind is in the hands of his children. Peter, you have four of them, so please put on your… thinking cap."

Lourdes chuckled. "A curious expression, but I understand. Have you met any of Peter's children?"

"I worked with his daughter Denise for years at the library and we are good friends."

Her lips twitched mischievously. "Were you her boss?"

"No, I was only a library assistant. She's the librarian," I said with a sense of relief, as that was one revelation ticked off my lengthy list.

"He's also spoken to my son Simon on the phone several times."

"Is he the interfering one?"

"Yes, and part of the reason why Richie came here, but he can tell you about that himself."

Thanks a million, chum, I thought, though he was only laying the groundwork for the full confession of my sins that I knew would happen quite soon. I sensed that Lourdes wouldn't be too bothered about my past life, because she'd obviously met plenty of successful men and not been overly impressed by mere material gain. Peter then said something that revealed a spot of groundwork that he'd already indulged in.

After a prolonged titter during which I believe he was weighing up the pros and cons of what he was about to say, he came out with the following cracker.

"You know, Lourdes, in some ways I find it quite ironic that your father and my son are both involved in car dealing."

Rather than looking perplexed, as I'd anticipated, she nodded gravely and said that in this life truth was often stranger than fiction. I believe they would have then shared a good old cackle, had Lourdes been the cackling kind, but instead she screwed up her eyes and patted her lips with a paper napkin.

"I must get back to pick up Alberto from his football match," she said, before I snatched the bill from her grasp and told her the lunch would be my treat.

I think the memory of her lips on my cheeks and her hand on my side, just below the rib cage, tempered my annoyance with my pal as he drove us back to town, though I did grunt and groan a bit as he cackled to his heart's content.

"Well, Richie, you did once say that it'll all come out in the wash in the end, so all I've done is set the timer."

"I think you've already done the pre-wash, mate, though I suppose I should be grateful."

"No point in beating about the bush with a shrewd lass like Lourdes."

"But that bit about the car dealing was... I mean, what was that about?"

"Oh, I happened to call in at the health centre the other day while you were studying. We stepped outside and had a chinwag, you know. Just a bit of idle conjecture about this and that really."

"Does she know that Simon's paying me to be here?"

"Yes."

"Did you suggest that her dad might... find me useful in some way?"

"Yes."

"I see. Right, er... don't you think you were putting the cart before the horse, or the cars before the girl a bit there, Peter?"

He shrugged. "I don't see what one thing necessarily has to do with the other. I mean, Lourdes is already a pal of yours, so why shouldn't she suggest you to her dad as a possible assistant?"

Put in that cleverly logical way, I saw that he hadn't risked my future happiness after all. As for helping Lourdes's dad to sell his vehicles to foreign millionaires, well, I spoke excellent English, would soon improve my Spanish, and also had a smattering of French. Although supercars didn't interest me in the least, I had a mind capable of absorbing a sufficient amount of information about them in a relatively short time to be able to impress most punters. I was, according to Denise and one or two other people, a pleasant and communicative sort of guy, and although I hadn't done much selling, I assumed that Lourdes's dad would take care of that side of things.

I then lamented that I'd struggle to get to El Puerto de Santa María or anywhere else the car dealer wished me to go.

"You can use my car until you buy your own."

"Thanks, but I haven't even started to do my residence paperwork yet."

"Then begin right away."

"Oh, what a bore."

He clicked his tongue. "Oh, dear, is the old Richie beginning to rear his idle head again?"

I straightened my slumping shoulders. "No, I'll do whatever it takes to impress Lourdes… and get on in life."

"One thing ought to lead to another, if you keep your wits about you and become the dynamic man who I believe you are deep down."

"Deep down, yes."

12 – A Crucial Meeting

Then things began to move faster than I'd expected. The following Wednesday Lourdes invited me to her flat in the evening to discuss a few matters, she'd said in her text, so I made my way to the seafront address not far from the lighthouse in a determined and not at all romantic frame of mind. Peter suspected that she'd wish to talk about my possible involvement in her father's lucrative hobby, and as my friend always seemed to be at least one step ahead of me, I felt fairly sure that she wouldn't greet me at the door dressed in a negligee.

In the event a handsome teenage boy greeted me at the door of the large, airy second-floor apartment dressed in a football strip.

"Hola, you must be Alberto."

"Yes, I'm Alberto, and you must be Richie," he said in English, but rather than retaliating in Spanish as I'd done on a couple of occasions when people had challenged my right to speak the lingo of the land, I humoured the lad as he peppered me with questions on our way through the lobby, hoping that he'd soon buzz off to play soccer and leave his mum and me alone.

He led me into a large living room and stood aside after opening a French window.

"Good luck," he said as he closed it from within and gave me a thumbs up sign.

On the long balcony with a marvellous sea view I saw not the future love of my life, but a balding, heavyset man leaning over a low table and peering at an iPad. He was dressed in an expensive-looking shirt and trousers, shiny brown shoes, and wore a Rolex watch on his thick hairy wrist, but he still somehow looked as if he'd just walked in from the fields.

"Take a seat, Rishie," he said in Spanish without looking up.

I complied.

He switched off the tablet and turned his dark jowly face towards me. "Got a Frenchman in Estepona who can't decide if he wants the F430 or the 328 GTS. What do you make of that?" he said in a deep lispy voice that I just about understood.

As luck and a healthy dose of fortuitous foresight had it, I'd already made a preliminary study of the supercar market and had found myself fascinated by the vast array of Ferraris which had been made over the years. A few days earlier I could only have named the Testarossa, but I was now able to make an educated guess as to what he was driving at.

"Er, the 328 GTS is much older, isn't it?"

He grinned grimly. "Yes, a real eighties classic, while the F430 is more modern and far more powerful. Not comparable at all." He shrugged. "Maybe he just likes buying from me because he knows I'm not a crook. He's already got bored of the Porsche I sold him, the silly gabacho," he said, gabacho being a derogatory term for a Frenchman.

"Hmm. Is Lourdes out?"

"Eh? Oh, gone shopping or something. Anyway, the gabacho speaks Spanish, so I'll not need you to come, but I've got a Russian who's interested in a Maserati Spyder that I've got. Do you know that one?"

"Oh, they made a lot of Spyders over the years."

"This one's a Spyder Zagato from 1990. An ugly thing really, more like a Lancia, but this Russian's a poor sort of bloke compared to some of his countrymen. I'll need you to come with me to Fuengirola next week, if you can manage it."

"Yes, I can," I said, as he didn't seem like the sort of man who'd want to be bothered by petty logistical matters, such as how we were going to get home if he sold the car.

"Good. You can drive it there and I'll follow you in my Golf. Don't look so worried. It's like a Seat 600 compared to some of my cars." He laughed throatily and held out his hand. "Juan Manuel. Juanma to you."

I pressed his meaty paw firmly. "Ric*h*ie. Encantado."

He narrowed his brown eyes. "So, Rishie, you're the latest bloke to have designs on my daughter, are you?" I think he said, though his piercing look made the nature of his enquiry clear enough.

I smiled. "We met not long ago, through a mutual friend."

"Ah, the old Englishman she's told us so much about, but aren't you related?"

"No, but he's become like a fa… an older brother to me. I have come to Spain to try to–"

"Yes, yes, there'll be time enough to talk about that. Did you see the car on the street outside?"

"Er, I saw several."

"The only real car there, though it's a pile of junk if you ask me." When he pushed himself up I was surprised to see that he was only around five foot six, as he'd seemed larger physically as well as larger than life, though I suspected that his blustery manner was merely a means to avoid talking about things that didn't interest him, like me.

"Oh, the red Jaguar."

"Yes, an XKR from 1999, made after they'd forgotten how to make real cars like they used to do back in the fifties and sixties. I took it in part-exchange for a superb BMW, soft-hearted fool that I am, and it's been taking up space in my unit for the last two years."

"It looks nice and sporty from up here."

"Do you know what the Germans say about Jaguars?"

"No."

"By all means buy one, but keep a Golf in your garage for when it breaks down. Ha ha, I like that, me having a Golf in the garage." After rooting around in a trouser pocket, he handed me a set of keys. "It's yours for just fifteen thousand."

I held the keys like a metallic hot potato. "Oh, I can't afford a car like that… Juanma."

I heard a sliding sound.

"He really means that you're to take the car and try to sell it," said my saviour, looking lovely in a light checked jacket and blue jeans.

"Hola, Lourdes," I exhaled.

Rather than giving me the two kisses I anticipated, she sat down in a wicker chair opposite her father and poured herself a glass of water.

"That is what you mean, isn't it, Papá?"

"Course I do. I wouldn't sell a piece of junk like that to my worst enemy, let alone to your agreeable new friend."

I'd remained by the balcony rail and on viewing the Jag again I began to salivate lightly. Just imagine me in such a cool set of wheels! If I sent my mum and sister a pic of Lourdes seated by my side in it, they'd really believe that I'd landed on my feet for once.

"Er, Juanma, why do you say it is a piece of junk?"

"Oh, it's not that bad really, but like most people I prefer Italian and German sports cars. You'll have your work cut out to sell it, but you can keep anything you get over fifteen thousand, which won't be much. It's a four-litre automatic with a lot of kilometres on the clock, you see, and that puts most folk off, though the few people who get to enter my unit scarcely give it a second glance."

Lourdes smiled and beckoned to me, so I sat down by her side.

"Think of it as a kind of test, Richie. Papá is fond of putting people on the spot like that."

Papá sniggered. "Selling cars is a tough business. Oh, I could get shut of it in no time, if I tried, but the women in my life insist that I take it easy these days."

"You should play golf more, Papá."

"I played the other day, but I ended up talking cars as usual. The trouble is that the stuck-up Andaluces I know at the club haven't really got two pesetas to rub together, not compared to the Russians and whatnot." He reached around the table and squeezed my knee. "We'll have a good time, you and me, making them part with the roubles they've made by fair means or foul," is a rough translation of what he said, though I understood most of his colloquial speech.

"Yes, it will be interesting for me."

"Have you worked in car sales before?"

"No."

"Good, because you won't have any preconceived ideas about how it's done. I once took on a young chap who'd worked for the Renault dealership in Cádiz, a distant relation of mine."

"Papá, Raul's your nephew."

"Yes, but he's in Tenerife now, trying his luck with the guiris (a derogatory word for Brits and other northern Europeans), the poor sap. I gave him a free hand and he tried to sell my cars in the usual way, you see, boring the punters with technical jargon and stuff like that, instead of sussing them out and finding that *one* small detail that'll clinch the deal."

"Such as what?" I asked.

"Well, an old Austrian bird got in touch with me once, and as I'd been told she was loaded I sent a nice-looking lad to fetch her from Marbella in a Bentley I happened to have at the time. So she comes into the unit with a daft little dog on a lead and starts looking around without a clue what she's after. Well, I was worried that the mutt would piss on my carpet and I'd blow my top at the sunburnt old dame."

"Papá's unit is fully carpeted, you see, apart from the workshop section," Lourdes managed to slot in.

"That damned Jaguar of yours leaked oil on it once, but the gasket's been changed now. Where was I? Oh, yes, so she's traipsing around with that dog of hers, criticising cars that she hasn't a clue about, then I notice that an Aston Martin I had on loan from a bent geezer from one of those Stan countries the Russians used to own…"

"Kazakhstan, Papá."

"That's the one. Anyway, I noticed that the upholstery was the same greenish colour as the dog's collar, so I bundled her into the driver's seat, stuck the mutt on the passenger seat, and showed her how well her little darling would look as she drove around Monaco, as that's where she had her main house, she told me." He drank some water, smacked his lips, and gazed at me.

"So did she buy it?"

"No, but it got her thinking about colours, so she ended up buying a Porsche 911, because it had brown seats that were just the same tone as her Filipino servant's skin, or so she said. It just goes to show, eh?"

"Er, yes."

Lourdes giggled. "It just goes to show that you can't always believe my father's car stories, but it keeps him out of mischief and he enjoys relieving these millionaires of their money."

He raised his hands and let them fall. "It's tough work, but someone has to do it, and it's my duty to keep their filthy lucre in Spain rather than have them waste it elsewhere. Right, got to get back for supper, or your mother will give me a tongue-lashing. Will we be seeing you on Sunday, love?"

"Yes."

"Bring Ricardo along, if you like."

"Richie, Papá."

"Rishie, yes."

"Ri*ch*ie."

"That's what I said, Rishie."

"I don't mind you calling me Ricardo," I said, as it sounded like a good name for a guy who whizzed around in supercars.

"Right, so I'll see you on Sunday, Ricardo." He gave his daughter a hug and a kiss on the forehead, drolly looked me up and down, then left.

I slumped into my chair and spotted the Jaguar's keys. "Oh, how is he going to get home?"

"His mechanic brought the Jaguar."

"Oh, so that's how sure he… you were that I'd take the car, is it?"

She ruffled my hair before sitting down opposite me. "The mechanic waited in the bar until Alberto told him he could go."

"And how did your son know that I'd take the car?"

"He used his judgement."

"I see. Hang on though. How did the mechanic get back to El Puerto de Santa María then?"

"He didn't. He lives here in Chipiona."

"Right. So how will he get to work tomorrow?"

"Ricardo... no, I much prefer Richie. Richie, if you're going to work for my father, you oughtn't to worry your head about minor details like that."

"No."

"With him you'd better go with the flow (dejarse llevar) and not concern yourself with the... financial ins and out of the business too much."

"Vale," I said, meaning OK.

"Papá swears that he always does things legally, but I know that a lot of cash changes hands during many of his transactions."

"Right. And is that strictly legal?"

"If my father deposits the final amount in his bank account and later declares his earnings, it is as far as he's concerned, but who's to know how some of these rich foreigners have made their money?" She sighed. "In a way this is right at the other end of the spectrum from the work you've been doing with the migrants. The kind of person who does one of these things wouldn't normally wish to do the other, if you see what I mean."

I pictured Demba clinging to Abdou's back, then the shiny red Jag on the street outside.

"Yes, I do see what you mean, but in my... delicate economic position, I think I should at least try to help your father sell some cars, don't you?"

"Of course you must give it a go."

I smiled timidly. "And what do you think of the kind of person who accepts money every month to look after an elderly man who is perfectly fit?"

She smiled brightly. "Circumstances dictate these things, and I've a feeling you won't be needing Peter's children's money for much longer."

I tapped the tabletop. "Let's hope not."

A while later when Lourdes had seen me to the door, I found my first goodbye kiss heading straight for her lips, but she turned her head and it landed softly on her cheek.

"Not just yet, Richie."

"Vale. See you on Sunday then."

"Sí, hasta el domingo."

There's only so much dialogue even an avid reader can stand, so I'll spare you the comical exchange between Peter and me when I called to ask him how to drive an automatic car. I was all for him coming to get me and my costly potential meal ticket, but he told me not to be soft and just stick it in D for drive.

"With what you're getting into now, you're going to have to be a bit more daring, son."

"I know."

So on arriving home I bravely stuck it in N for neutral, locked the car, and walked up the path feeling like a million soon-to-be-laundered euros.

13 – A Hasty Business

The very next day Peter and I got down to the urgent business of selling the Jaguar. He agreed with Juanma that it wouldn't be easy to shift, because posh cars of a certain age often reach the low point of their value before beginning to acquire classic status. A spot of online research had shown me that dealers were asking up to twenty-five grand for XKRs in a similar condition, but Peter pointed out that they could afford to bide their time, whereas I ought to go for a quick killing in order to make a positive first impression on my prospective employer.

I smiled at my cornflakes. "First impressions again."

"Yes, he'll be glad to get shut of that white... red elephant, and he needn't know how little profit you've made."

"You know I'm a poor liar, Peter."

"Then you'd better get some practice, because in that game total honesty is rarely the best policy, especially the shady way that Lourdes's dad goes about it."

"But Lourdes says he declares all his earnings."

"Sure, eventually, but plenty of cash will have changed hands along the way, especially with these mafioso types who you hear so much about these days."

"So do you think it might be slightly immoral for me to do this?"

He shrugged. "If it helps you to get a start in life, I can't see much wrong with it, as you're not the one who's made the money in some underhand way."

"A start in life at nearly forty-seven," I murmured.

Peter suggested that we print a couple of ads to stick in the car's windows and asked me how much I hoped to get for the tidy Jag with a mere 122,000 kilometres on the clock. I told him that although a quick sale may have its advantages, from then on Juanma might only pay me a daily rate for my assistance, so if I could make six or seven grand in one fell swoop, I'd be able to put an end to my immoral earnings from his son Simon right away. Peter opined that Juanma would be willing to share his profits to some extent, especially if I ended up being his only daughter's prospective husband, so he suggested a bargain basement price of €19,900.

I gasped. "But that'd be giving it away."

He shook his head. "Twenty grand is a lot of money for an old car that isn't especially sought after in this country. Just imagine if you could go to lunch on Sunday and tell your boss that you'd already sold it."

"Oh, boy, even he'd be impressed if I did that."

"Which is why you'll let it go for eighteen, if need be."

"A measly three grand profit," I mumbled.

"That'll mean three less months of having to invent cock and bull stories about my exercise obsession to Simon."

I recalled our last tiresome conversation on the phone and smiled. "By the end of the year I could tell him you're cured, then I'd be a free man at last."

"Exactly. Right, we'll be off in half an hour."

"Where to?"

He grinned. "There's only one place to take a car like that."

A while later we were cruising smoothly along the familiar road south, but this time we purred past the campsite and turned right before reaching the splendid Playa de Punta Candor. As well as the usual morning strollers, we saw a few large purplish people sunbathing in spite of the wind, for we were now close to Rota, home of the Hispano-American naval base which Peter had failed to visit several years earlier. He told me that up to six thousand Americans lived in the area, about half of them on active duty and the rest civilian employees and family members.

"And as far as I know, the Yanks still like Jaguars, so let's try to draw a bit of attention to ourselves and the car," he said as he bluetacked an A4 ad to the passenger door that faced the entrance to the carpark.

"And how will we do that, pray?"

"By clowning around and taking a few photos."

"Oh, I forgot my camera."

He sniggered. "The Olympus that you simply had to have?" He passed me his rucksack. "They're both in there."

Our first act of clowning was to snap each other behind the wheel, before Peter took the liberty of popping his camera on the roof of a nearby Seat and setting the timer to capture us both, with the advert out of sight, of course. As a crowd of car aficionados failed to gather around us, we soon went for a stroll along the beach, until I received a call from an American fellow and we hotfooted it back to the car. The caller proved to be a muscly young marine called Danny who liked the look of the Jag and thought it a steal at the price, but unfortunately he was due to be posted back to the States in two months' time. He promised to spread the word among his colleagues, before saluting – out of habit, we presumed – and speeding away on a powerful Honda motorbike.

I spat out a few stray grains of sand. "Ah, if only I had more time to sell it."

"The day's still young. Let's drive on to the town's beaches. We might see other guys like him with money to burn."

The compact town of Rota has a small beach facing the Atlantic, and just past the pretty harbour another golden strip along the bay opposite the naval base in which we could discern three grey ships that Peter believed to be a corvette and a couple of missile or patrol boats. Possibly because of our proximity to their workplace, we saw few American-looking people on either beach, so we parked up near the port, attached both ads to the side windows, and headed into the unremarkable town centre, as Rota was a mere fishing village until Franco invited the US Navy to make themselves at home there.

"Red Jag for sale, red Jag for sale," I sang sotto voce as we strolled through the small main square, causing only a dozing mongrel to prick up its ears. "Oh, I wish I had more time to sell the damned thing." I came to a halt by a burbling little fountain. "But I *do* have more time. It's preposterous to think I'm going to sell it right away, so I might as well enjoy it till someone buys it."

Peter chuckled. "Enjoy it? You drive it like an old granny."

"I'm scared I'll damage it in some way. I'm not that happy about leaving it on your street either, but I've got no choice. If some jealous youth decides to scratch it, I'll end up hundreds of euros down. It's a great responsibility having a car like that."

"Let's have a coffee, then we'll shoot the other arrow I've got in my quiver."

"What's that?"

"You'll see."

So after a quick caffeine boost we removed the adverts and I allowed Peter to take the wheel. He swiftly drove us to a car dealership on the outskirts of town, where a friendly fellow called Alejandro greeted him warmly, him being one of his Chipiona mates who hadn't become estranged due to the migrant business, assuming he knew about it, which most people appeared to do. After asking after the man's family, Peter got down to brass tacks and told him in rather vague terms why I had to sell the Jaguar quickly. Alejandro walked around the now dusty vehicle, even kicking a tyre as one does in these situations, before saying that if I could leave it with him for a few weeks, he was confident that he'd get me twenty thousand for it. This sounded good to me, as the car would be safe in the showroom, and if he were true to his word, I'd make enough money to enable me to retire from my caring duties right away.

"Me parece una muy buena idea," I told him, before indicating that Peter could now hand over the keys.

My friend had been assessing Alejandro's reaction to the car, he later told me, and then took it upon himself to ask him if he wouldn't rather buy the car now and thus increase his prospective profits.

The suave man's brows rose on hearing this, before his dark eyes became positively hawklike. He ambled around the Jag again, kicking a different tyre, before telling Peter that to take such a risk with the dealership's money, his friend would have to give him a substantial discount.

"Eighteen thousand," I said.

He shooed away the keys that Peter proffered and shook his head. "Too much. Look, I have all these lovely Hyundais to sell, so why should I take a big risk on a tired old Jaguar?"

"It's not tired," I protested. "It's... it's just getting going."

He sniggered. "A lot of kilometres to get going, no? Look, if you want a quick sale I can give you fourteen thousand for it today. Otherwise I can only try to sell it on your behalf, which won't be easy."

"You said you were confident that you could get twenty within a few weeks."

He smiled. "I'm a born optimist, but at this time of year, with fewer Americans at the base and no tourists, it may take longer."

"He'll take fifteen," said P.

"Hey, I–"

"Fifteen I can do."

"But…"

"He'll need to get the owner's signature."

"Er…"

"Vale, let's step into my office and I'll take your friend's bank details."

"I'll give you mine, as he hasn't opened an account yet," Peter said as they moved away.

Alejandro looked over his shoulder at the stunned guiri. "Here in Spain for a short time and already competing with the likes of me, eh? Peter, your friend is a born entrepreneur."

"Yes, he has a great nose for a deal."

"What deal?" I wailed. "Hang on a minute, you two."

They stopped and perused me patiently, before Peter wagged a finger at me.

"Richie, please think about the bigger picture. We'll wait for you inside."

So they walked on, patting and pushing each other like two best buddies on a night out, while I stood rooted to the spot, trying to focus on the bigger picture. In it Juanma loomed large, his Rolex gleaming on his hairy wrist, while Lourdes stood by his side, illuminated by a celestial-type light – not unlike Our Lady of Lourdes, I later reflected – and beckoning me into their world.

"I still think I've been diddled," I moaned to Peter after Alejandro had driven us back to Chipiona at great speed in his bargain supercar.

"How can you have been diddled if you didn't have a damned thing in the first place?"

"But I've made a net profit of zero-point-zero."

"You've done as you were told and freed up floorspace in your future father-in-law's unit."

"Hmm."

"And he needn't know that you only got fifteen for it. The money's going into my bank account, remember, and from there into his, unless he wants cash, in which case he'll have to come to the bank with me, as you'd have kittens if you had to look after so much money." He looked up at the lighthouse and scratched his bronzed bald patch. "Tell him you got eighteen. That's believable enough."

"I won't be able to lie to him and Lourdes."

"Then tell Lourdes the truth and just lie to him."

"But she's his daughter, you… ninny."

"From what you've told me, all this is just a big game for him, so play the game and have a bit of fun while you're feathering your nest."

"I'll see what she says."

"OK. Now buy me lunch to celebrate your success."

I patted my still slim wallet. "All right."

14 – A Constructive Sunday

"Of course I can keep your sordid secret," Lourdes said as we approached the mythical industrial unit at about noon on yet another sunny Sunday. "And Peter's right. Papá would be disappointed if you'd only got what he wanted for the car, although he may not even ask you how much you made."

"Really?"

"That's your business after all. Just be cagey about it, so he can amuse himself trying to guess, though he might not give it a second thought if he has other things on his mind. Here we are."

After passing several business units of various sizes, we'd pulled into the weedy carpark of a smallish beige-coloured one which didn't appear to have any windows. Close to a dusty green VW Golf I saw a battered little Peugeot, and all in all the place looked forlorn and neglected. The dirty metal shutters had been raised just high enough to allow a short person to access the heavy doors within which a dusky uniformed guard was stationed. This large, hatchet-faced young man appeared to be about to hug me.

"You don't have to search him, Khalid. He's my friend."

"The boss says I have to, Señorita Lourdes."

She frowned. "How silly."

"He says he doesn't trust any Englishmen."

So I raised my arms and allowed myself to be so thoroughly frisked that he ended up prodding me uncomfortably close to my private parts.

"What's this, Señor?"

"My keys."

"Vale, you can go in." He grinned at Lourdes. "The boss says we're going to get one of those metal detectors, like in the airport."

She tutted. "That's just like him, always trying to dramatize things."

Another heavy pair of doors began to open automatically and we gradually beheld the boss, looking not at all businesslike in a scruffy blue polo shirt, grubby grey trousers, and leather sandals.

"The metal detector will be mainly to impress the Russians. A couple of blokes who came here carried guns under their jackets, you see, and sort of swaggered around as if I wasn't supposed to know it, though it was pretty damned obvious. They were just underlings, of course, sent to take a peek at what I've got, so they'll get beeped at next time, ha ha."

"Did you understand all that, Richie?"

"More or less, but didn't they get searched?" I patted my upper thigh. "Like I did."

She chuckled. "Khalid is quite new too, as is his cousin Samir who does the night shift." She kissed the boss. "Papá's always thinking of new ways to add mystique to his hobby."

After shaking Juanma's hand I was able to turn my attention to the contents of the unit. There were about twenty cars in there, most of them barely visible in the dim light, until he flicked some switches and lit up the scene like an especially bright Hollywood film set.

"Wow," I said obligingly as I looked at the four rows of vehicles, with the Italian supercars and the Porsches in places of prominence and the boring BMWs, Mercs and other utilitarian cars towards the back. "It's quite a collection," I said eagerly, though if truth be told the sight of so much ostentatious hardware didn't thrill me all that much.

Juanma took my arm and led me to an empty space right at the back.

"See that stain on the carpet there? Your Jaguar did that, and even though it's been fixed, it's not coming back."

I feigned a yawn which I politely stifled. "Oh, I've sold that one."

He perused my languid eyes. "Oh… good."

"I'll need you to sign the papers, and if you give me your bank details, I'll transfer the money tomorrow."

He eyed me suspiciously. "So they didn't pay in cash then?"

I shrugged like a young Marlon Brando on being invited into bed by a gorgeous girl. "We-ell, I'm new to this game and I'm not sure what the counterfeiters get up to in Spain, so I insisted on fifteen thousand through the bank, and the… well, that seemed like the best idea at the time," I said, trotting out a line that I'd rehearsed but didn't really think I'd have the confidence to utter.

Still a bit stunned, I believe, he fiddled with an Audi A5's wing mirror for a while, before saying that he'd need the fifteen in cash, as a poverty-stricken Pole in Puente Genil was desperate to sell a nice old four-seater Porsche 911 designed by Pininfarina. The fact that his speech was also alliterative in Spanish suggested that he'd been making it up as he went along, something that his daughter's wry smile seemed to confirm. The bit about the armed Russians might have been poppycock too, along with more of his tales, but it was an undeniable fact that his unprepossessing unit contained cars worth a heck of a lot of money, though I knew by then that his Italian supercars were all lower-end models rather than the kind that fetch millions at auction.

"Right, you've seen what you're going to be helping me to sell, so let's go home for lunch," he said, and until the end of the day we made no further reference to my sale or the fifteen thousand that I was going to have to get out of Peter's bank account and guard with my life until I handed it over.

It turned out that a completely different subject was about to dominate out lunchtime conversation, because after Lourdes had introduced me to her kindly, refined mother from whom she'd undoubtedly inherited her looks and fine breeding, Juanma brought up the thorny subject of Miguel Ángel, his daughter's errant ex-husband.

"Oh, Papá, do we really have to talk about him?" she said at the large oval table in the spacious dining room of the modern flat which overlooked the famed Paseo Marítimo on the western edge of the city, with a marvellous view of the Atlantic.

"During Ricardo's first lunch with us too," said María Isabel, indicating that I'd made a decent first impression, so far.

Juanma speared a stick of asparagus and munched it savagely, soon emptying his mouth enough to say that an old pal of his might have provided the means to getting shut of that annoying little shit once and for all.

"He is your grandchildren's father, Papá."

"More's the pity." He dabbed a bit of oil from his chin. "Anyway, my mate Eduardo who I've known since we did the mili (military service) together still lives in Huelva and him and his brothers have a fishing boat they want to sell. My idea is to gift it to that son of... his mother, on the condition that he buggers off to live there."

"But his–" Lourdes began.

"Oh, he can keep his boat in Chipiona, as I believe his crew will run the show better without that drunken sot around."

"I was about to say that his son lives in Chipiona, with me, and his daughter spends her holidays there."

"Bah, it's not like I'm sending him to Mexico, much as I'd like to. It's only a couple of hours' drive away, and he can keep that crappy flat he's renting if he wants, but the main thing is that he'll be out of your hair during the week, every week, as I'll stipulate in a *legal* contract that he's not to show his face in Chipiona between Monday and Friday, and he's not to bother you at all. It'll be my own personal restraining order and just as valid as a real one." He gazed at our perturbed faces. "So what do you think of that?"

"You can't just–" Lourdes began again.

"No, I'd like to hear what Ricardo thinks of my idea first."

As I hadn't been able to rehearse a speech in response to this totally unexpected turn of events, I took my time chewing a slice of cured ham, before saying the first thing that came into my head.

"It might be good for him to get away from Chipiona… and start a new life elsewhere." I shrugged. "It's what I'm doing, and so far it's going very well."

"He may mend his ways in Huelva, God willing," said María Isabel.

"But you can't just buy people off like that, Papá," said his disgruntled daughter.

"Want to bet? Do you know how much a boat like that with its own place on the quayside costs? And with a competent crew who'll help him to make a lot of money, if he doesn't mess things up again. Oh, mark my words, the grasping little git will jump at the chance. Besides, Ricardo's right about him needing to start afresh somewhere else."

He drank half a glass of wine, before slapping the left side of his chest. "I'm getting too old to be worrying about a twerp like that ruining my darling daughter's life."

"He's not–"

"Ha, he'll take the bait all right… sorry, you were saying?"

"He's not exactly ruining my life, Papá. He's just being annoying from time to time."

I straightened up and raised my fork. "One day soon I intend to have a chat with Miguel Ángel. We will talk things over man to man. I believe he will see reason and stop bothering Lourdes."

The family exchanged glances, pensive pouts, and noncommittal side-to-side head movements, before Lourdes cleared her throat.

"Papá, you may speak to Miguel Ángel about your generous offer, but please don't try to force him to move."

Her mother nodded. "Yes, viewed objectively, I believe your proposal may well please him, so you have my blessing to discuss it with him."

I lay down my fork and sipped my alcohol-free beer. My input seemed to have done the trick, and that was all that mattered.

After a delicious, mainly fish-based lunch that I won't bother to describe, Juanma personally refilled my coffee cup and told me we'd be taking the Maserati Spyder to Fuengirola on Thursday to show it to the impoverished Russian who needed a cheap set of wheels.

"Vale, I will meet you at the unit in Peter's car and follow you there."

He grinned. "Don't you want to drive the Spyder?"

"Oh, I don't mind either way."

"Hey, why don't you bring the old Englishman along? I've heard a lot about him and I'd like to meet him."

I strove to hide a delighted smile by scratching my nose. "All right, I'll see if he wants to come."

"You do that."

"And we… I'll fetch your cash."

"Eh? Oh, that. OK, I've got a safe at the unit."

"That's good."

"Don't pretend that you aren't relieved that Peter's going to be holding your hand on Thursday," Lourdes said as she drove us smoothly home in the Audi which had indeed been a gift from her parents.

"Eh? Oh, I thought he might enjoy a day out."

"Yes, but don't let him steal the show, or Papá may reward him instead of you."

"Oh, Peter has always had my best interests at heart. After all, without him where would I be now?"

She squeezed my hand. "Still in your cold, damp country, instead of here by my side."

Things were looking up in all respects.

15 – The End is Nigh…

On Tuesday we read in the Diario de Cádiz newspaper that a patera had been intercepted near Conil de la Frontera with thirty-two migrants on board. Conil is about fifty miles to the south of Chipiona, so Søren believed that it might have been a new route which the smugglers would ditch in favour of our tried and tested strip of coastline, now that the patrols had diminished and we hadn't heard a helicopter for several nights. After trying and failing to contact the cooperative smuggler, however, Søren feared that he must have been a member of the captured crew, a theory that passing time seemed to confirm, because neither he nor Elise – soon to return from her self-imposed exile – heard from him again.

At the time it seemed to herald the definitive end of Peter's endeavours and I felt glad that I'd been privileged to take part in my single memorable escapade. My friend wasn't too disappointed to miss out on one final pickup and turned his attention to planning the trip to Dakar which he intended to make no later than April, when the weather would still be relatively mild there. I still fancied the idea of accompanying him, though that would depend on the longevity of my car-dealing career, and to a lesser extent on the state of play between Lourdes and me, because although we were yet to become intimate, I believed we were both sure that we had a future together, and she wasn't the kind of woman who would begrudge me a month or so under African skies.

"Lourdes won't begrudge me a month or so under African skies," I said to Peter as he piloted the powerful Maserati Spyder along the east-bound motorway towards the Costa del Sol, with Juanma close behind in my friend's Ford.

"No, but you'll have to see how this car-dealing caper pans out."

"I foresee me making enough to give me a bit of breathing space, then leaving Juanma to it."

He chuckled. "Juanma doesn't look like the kind of bloke who'll let his daughter's consort go if he proves to be good at this sort of thing."

"Do you think I will be?"

"Frankly, no, because you're simply not the salesman type, but I reckon that Juanma, and probably his missus too, want to give you a start in li… Spain, so that you'll be able to fend for yourself and decide what you really want to do."

I stretched up to feel the wind in my hair, as Peter had insisted on taking the top down. "I wonder what I'll really want to do."

"Whatever it is, I think you'll be able to count on some help from your bruiser of a father-in-law."

"Er, me and Lourdes haven't even kissed yet."

"All in good time."

"Maybe I'll ask him for a fishing boat, then go and ply my… nets in the Atlantic."

"You wouldn't last a week."

"I know. I got seasick during a cruise on Lake Windermere once. Anyway, enough dreaming about the future. What's our game plan with this starving Russian buyer then?"

"To keep our mouths shut until Juanma invites us to open them."

"That suits me."

And that's the way it proved to be, because on the driveway of a large but dilapidated chalet on the outskirts of Fuengirola, Juanma did all the talking and the mature Ukrainian – the same as a Russian, according to Juanma – listened patiently with his tanned armed folded and his double chin resting on his barrel chest. When he finally spoke, it was with the brusqueness of a Slavic baddie in an American film.

"You say thirty-five, but I say this car is worth no more than twenty-five," he said in passable Spanish.

"But it's a Maserati, Andrey."

He scoffed. "It looks more like a Lancia to me."

"I can let this beautiful car go for thirty-two, but no less."

He shook his head. "I don't haggle. I have twenty-five thousand ready for you, in used notes, so you can take them or leave them."

Juanma had confessed to us that he intended to get shut of the car that day, as he really wanted to buy a 1970s Rolls Royce – not a Porsche 911 Pininfarina – from a Spanish, rather than Polish, seller in Puente Genil. I believe he was about to accept the Ukrainian's offer when Peter began to shuffle around the car, rubbing his chin and apparently engaged in a tortuous thought-process which perplexed us all, because since reaching the house he hadn't opened his mouth, and when Juanma had given me a brisk pep talk outside, he'd wandered into some nearby bushes to have a pee.

As Peter pottered around it dawned on me that the Ukrainian had no idea why he was there, so when my friend began to root in his deep shorts pocket I had a feeling that he was about to shake things up a bit. Sure enough, after coming to a halt by the front bumper, he first faced the sun and grimaced, before plunging his hand into the pocket and pulling out a big wad of banknotes.

"All right, Juanma, I'll give you the twenty-eight," he muttered in Spanish.

Innocent Richie was flabbergasted, of course, and old Andrey looked puzzled and more than a little disgruntled, but Juanma rose to the occasion like a champion salesman.

"*Now* you tell me that, you…" He growled. "Look, you've missed your chance, so put that money away." He looked at the current punter and shook his head. "I'm sorry, but these Englishmen really don't know how to comport themselves."

"Then why the devil is he here?" the big man growled.

"Ricardo, why is he here?"

"Er, because I agreed to drive him into town afterwards," I said, as quick as a rather slow flash, but quick enough, it transpired.

Juanma then did a very good job of looking torn between grabbing the eccentric Brit's cash and rejecting his untimely bid, but a plaintive Slavic groan preceded a muttered offer to match the old pest's twenty-eight thou.

Juanma looked downcast. "I apologise once more for this... man's intrusion." He glared at me. "You and me will speak about this afterwards, Ricardo."

I whimpered something suitably subservient and turned away, fearing that my rising mirth might give the game away.

Juanma sighed. "If you prefer, I will return this afternoon, without these two... encumbrances, and we can resume our discussion."

"Come inside," he snapped, so off they went to do the deal.

"So you forgot to give Juanma the cash then?" I said to the gleeful Peter.

"Not exactly. Neither of you mentioned it, so I thought I'd hang onto it for a while longer. It gives me a warm feeling and... well, I had an inkling that it might come in handy."

"Hmm, you're either a born fraudster or a fabulous liar."

He smirked and shrugged. "He'd already shut the unit doors when I remembered, so I thought, what the hell, he can have it later. A stroke of luck, eh?"

"I'll say."

Juanma then emerged, patting his jacket pocket, and as our host failed to step outside to see us off, we were soon rolling down the hill in Peter's trusty Ford Focus.

"How about a bite to eat by the beach?" I said from the back seat.

"How about us nipping over to Puente Genil to snap up that Rolls?" said Juanma, so we nipped northwards just short of a hundred miles, stopping for a speedy lunch at a roadside bar, before tracking down the sixty-something Spanish owner of the gleaming blue car which he'd hired out for weddings during the decade that he'd owned it.

You may or may not know that Rolls Royce lowered their standards and upped their production in the seventies and eighties, so cars from that era command surprisingly low prices. Juanma had told us that he was happy to pay twelve thousand if the car was as good as the owner had claimed, and as it turned out to be even better, my boss was all for handing over the cash and driving it home (as his tailored insurance policy covered any car from 1946 to the present day, curiously enough).

The Spaniard seemed like a laid-back sort of fellow and his smart chalet plus the newish Volvo which stood beside the Rolls on the drive suggested that he wasn't short of a bob or two, so I decided it was finally time to make my presence felt, as I'd done nothing at all to earn my keep so far, apart from shelling out thirty euros for lunch. So it was that after indulging in a spot of pensive tyre kicking, I grumpily asserted that the tired old Rolls wasn't worth a cent over ten thousand, as Spain was littered with obsolete cars like that which no-one wanted.

The owner patiently heard me out, while Juanma's face showed neither approval nor disdain for my clumsy efforts. Peter had just wandered away to avoid laughing when the man finally stopped biting his lip and turned to face Juanma.

"Will you be paying cash?"

The boss patted his bulging jacket pocket. "Of course."

"Eleven thousand then. My final word."

They shook hands and went inside.

Within twenty minutes we were on the road, with a beaming Juanma following us in the Rolls which he ended up keeping for some time. After a quick pit stop on the outskirts of Utrera, the three motoring musketeers parted company for the day.

"I don't feel like I've earned it," I said to Peter as I counted the four thousand euros for the third time.

"The day's turned out just as we all wanted it to."

"You must accept the two thousand that Juanma gave you, though it should have been three."

"I want nowt out of today's enjoyable outing, though you can pay for the diesel and do one more thing that I assume you're going to do anyway."

"What's that?"

"Call my Simon and hand in your notice. Tell him I've given up climbing the lighthouse steps and packed in swimming for the winter. I now walk as slowly as an old man ought to, so I'm effectively cured."

"And will you give up the steps and the swimming?"

"Will I heck."

"Good." I stashed my ill-gotten gains and rubbed my hands together. "I can't wait to call him, and Denise too. Ah, free of my chains and with a clear conscience at last."

"Yes, until next Tuesday when you two take that Porsche to Marbella to sell to the… who was it? A Rumanian gangster?"

"So he says. Are you not going to come?"

"No, I've had my fun, and it's you Juanma wants to groom, at least until you're a bridegroom."

"Lourdes still only kisses me on the cheeks," I muttered. "It's getting a bit silly now, but if that's the way she wants it…"

"Then that's the way it has to be. Patience, my boy. By the sound of it you've had a lively love life compared to most people, so now that you've found the real thing, you ought to relish every step of the way."

"Yes, I will."

As far as we knew, Juanma was still in negotiations with his pal from Huelva regarding the fishing boat that he intended to give to Lourdes's ex-husband, but the day after we'd successfully sold the Porsche – and Juanma had thrust two thousand into my hand simply for making a couple of decisive comments, he claimed – the fisherman tripped over a rope on his boat and fell onto the quayside, smashing his left femur against a metal bollard. Lourdes's lovely daughter Rocío rushed home from Seville and spent hours at his bedside, often alternating with her brother Alberto, and Lourdes herself visited him a few times, urging him to give up the booze that he swore had had nothing to do with the fall, although one of his crew had told her that he'd been toting a hipflask for some time.

Even I popped my head around the door on one occasion, and after being introduced as a family friend, the swarthy invalid gazed at me grimly but without malice. The fracture had shaken him up badly and he seemed sincerely intent on mending his ways, so the yet-to-be-mentioned boat purchase was put on hold because, as Juanma said, there was no point in spending upwards of €60,000 if the annoying little son of a bitch was going to behave himself anyway – his words, not mine.

It was after leaving the hospital that day when Lourdes kissed me on the lips for the first time, possibly because her injured ex hadn't bawled out the man he must surely have known about by then. It seems appropriate to wind up with a few sweet nothings, but as we didn't utter any until some time later, I won't sully my almost wholly truthful account with a flurry of fibbing right at the end. I finally seemed to be on the road to some sort of success, so I'll finish on that happy note.

Thank you for having the patience to get this far. At the time of writing I'm nowhere near as idle as I used to be, but it's taken me a whole year to produce my story so far, so I'll be glad to give my right hand a rest, not to mention the pounding my poor fingertips have taken while typing it up on the computer. If I find myself with the time and the inclination, I'll go on with my story someday, but now I really need to have a lie down, so goodbye and God bless.

> Richie 'Ricardo' Bannister,
> Andalucía,
> January 2024

Printed in Great Britain
by Amazon